# Your Next Pastorate

## Starting the Search

by
RICHARD N. BOLLES
RUSSELL C. AYERS
ARTHUR F. MILLER
LOREN B. MEAD

AN ALBAN INSTITUTE PUBLICATION

The Publications Program of The Alban Institute is assisted by a grant from Trinity Church, New York City.

Library of Congress Catalog Card Number 90-83135.
ISBN #1-56699-041-6.

# CONTENTS

89794

# *How to Read This Book*

Begin with Bolles, **Chapter I: The Clergy Job Search: An Overview.** This may be the psychological starting point for your inquiry because it might be important for you to touch your anxieties about search committees, interviews, the job search process before moving to the *logical* starting point, which is...

**Chapter II: Build Your Search Around Your Giftedness,** by Arthur Miller. What do you enjoy and do well? Miller provides searching questions to help you get clear about what abilities shine forth from your specific achievements. Under what circumstances can you do your best work? What really motivates you? Your answers to Miller's careful questions will help you construct a picture of your ideal job and begin to answer the question "What church needs and wants your mix of gifts?"

Next, in **Chapter III**, look at your *choices* with Russell Ayers. Read **Section A, Identifying Choices amidst the Anxiety of the Job Search,** *unless* you are beginning the search in big trouble. In that case read **Section B, When a Clergyperson is in Serious Trouble.** Or unless you are dealing with a disability in which case **Section C, For the Clergyperson with Disability,** is for you. Ayers offers wise and empathic counsel tailored to your situation. He acknowledges the anxiety and other feelings that invariably accompany the job search and encourages you to get support and help when needed. What are your reasons for moving on? How can you move toward a helpful mindset and organize your resources for the search?

In **Chapter IV**, Loren Mead has some specific advice about **Getting Support: What Kind, Why, and How.** At this point you may want to return to the Bolles chapter about the job search itself, and particularly to the questions that concern you most.

Next move on to **Chapter V: What's the Matter With That Church
—Are They Stalling, or What?** by Loren Mead. You have been ab-
sorbed in your inner direction-finding. Now your search process bumps
up against some real people out there in a congregation who are engaged
in a search of their own. The disjunctures between your search process
and theirs may leave you frustrated, angry, and resentful. Mead lets you
in on the congregation's process and explains why it takes so much time.

Use the **Postscript: The Clergy Job-Hunt Check List** to make your
own check list for action, summarizing your notes and putting your plan
in a time frame.

This book began with the questions of clergy. Speed Leas listened for
these questions in his work with pastors, wrote them down, and sent
them to us. Other clergy submitted questions at our request. When we
sent the questions to Dick Bolles, he sent us some answers. We
encouraged other experts in career development to add their wisdom.
And so the book grew.

There are three things that I think are special about this book. First, the
congregational setting is clear. You don't have to translate general
career advice into the language of parish clergy. Second, this book opens
out lots of options, even for those who start out feeling their choices are
severely limited. Ayers and Bolles especially help the clergyperson not
to feel as though he or she were in a corner and to see that the future
extends many choices. Third, all these authors have attempted not only
to give good solid practical advice, but to ground it in their conviction
that God calls us to ministry, has given us gifts to use for the church, and
will be alongside us when the way is dark and we feel anxious,
despairing, or lost.

                                          Celia Allison Hahn, Editor

# CHAPTER I

# The Clergy Job Search:
# An Overview
# Questions from Clergy,
# Answers from Richard N. Bolles

**1. How do clergy learn to work with the system, but not be victimized by it?**

Generally speaking, calling committees or search committees are in the driver's seat these days as it is usually easier for them to find a pastor (though not necessarily a *good* pastor) than it is for the pastor to find a parish that wants them. This being in the driver's seat is characteristic of many secular organizations as well, and in their search behavior, many parishes are indistinguishable from secular organizations. The search committee imports the attitudes they forged in the workplace. Whatever they decide (like refusing to look at candidates who submit their own names) is going to be the case *in that parish*. What the clergy candidate needs to ask themself, however, is, "Why would I want to work in a parish like that?" The calling committee is deciding that assertive behavior is the mark of a bad clergyperson. With such judgmental behavior early on, one can prophesy a very tense relationship ever thereafter. It is an ancient rule in counseling that applies to all human behavior: "The microcosm reveals the macrocosm." How a parish behaves during the search process will reveal volumes about its ongoing life once the ordained leader is called. Hoping you can reform them, even with God's help, may be a most forlorn hope. (Cf. Jesus vis-a-vis the Pharisees.) The phenomenon is called "hardening of the heart." You will run into many hardened hearts during the search process. Weep for them, and then, as the Lord said, Shake the dust off your feet, and go on to a place that *will* receive you.

**2. How can I lessen my anxiety as I seek a new pastorate?**

Every clergyperson needs to know what else they could do besides working for the church. If you feel you *must* find employment in the church and only as a parish pastor or whatever, you will *always* be at a disadvantage in looking for a job. "No one is free until you have at least two things to choose between." You have a twin calling from God; find out what that other call is.

### 3. How can I think clearly about my vocational search?

Vocation is where what you most delight to do intersects with what God most needs to have done, as C. FitzSimons Allison many years ago observed.

### 4. What's the most important preparation for the job search?

You must know your talents backwards and forwards as a consequence of having done some truly *hard work* on inventorying your skills. (Cf. *Parachute* and Arthur Miller's chapter in this book.) Saying just off the top of your head, "Oh, I *know* what my talents are," is no longer sufficient in today's world.

### 5. After I've gotten clear about my skills, what are the next steps?

You must think out *very carefully (and in detail)* just what kind of church or place you want to serve and can most effectively serve, under God, and *only* take a call if it matches. There are other things you can do (Cf. #2 above). Taking any church just because you want to work in the church is just as bad as deciding to make pornography just because you want to eat. You won't do the ministry there well, and people will suffer, all in the name of your vocation. You certainly have the right to suffer for your own vocation, but no right to cause others to suffer for it. And if you've decided, like Abraham, to go out from where you are, do take the time to consult with every clergy friend you have to see if they've made a move recently or know someone who has. Then talk to those who have and pick their brains for everything they're worth, as to *how* they man-aged the move and secured the call. Particularly if it was to such a place as you are looking for, under God.

### 6. How should I answer written questions about my faith, my social action values, my life style values?

If a search committee asks you for answers to written questions about your faith, your social action values, and life style values, write your own answers (not those of some eloquent friend) and write as honestly as you can, without consideration of whether or not your answers will win you the post. God calls you to whatever place *He* genuinely calls you as *you are* (Cf. the hymn, "Just as I am....") Trying to pretend to be someone else, above all, trying to pretend to be The One you think the parish is looking for, is an ineffective way to search for a job in the secular world; in the church world, it's chicanery. The most important gift you have to offer them is God's Holy Spirit coming through *who you already are.* Dissembling about who you already are just for the sake of getting a job there is like burying your talent in the ground. And you know what our Lord thinks about *that.*

**7. What advice can you give me about how to answer the search committee's questions—especially difficult questions about my personal history?**

Remember, in giving answers to questions, the committee is not interested in your past *except as it may indicate things about the future.* In every answer you give, written or oral, ask yourself, How could I answer or explain this so as to reassure them about the future? You'll *have* to use your own words and thoughts, but the exchange might go something like this: e.g., *Search Committee*: "We notice you are divorced. Would you care to comment on how that will affect your ministry here?" *You to yourself*: "They're worried that in the future I will romance every single female/male in the parish, *or* they're worried that this is a sign I'm a quitter." *You to the Committee*: "My divorce was, above all else, a loss. A loss to me, a loss to my spouse, and a loss to all our friends. Its causes were very complex, but it was and is above all else a grief. But our Lord counsels us to put the past behind us and get on with serving Him. My primary preoccupation now is my vocation and my ministry. I think the fact that I'm divorced will pose no barrier to my doing a faithful ministry under God in this parish—except in the minds of those who are offended by divorce, particularly among clergy. And usually some parishioners are going to be offended by anyone you might call. There's no way you can cancel out people's prejudices. But the basis of my ministry is that I am a human being like all other humans, therefore a sinner, but one redeemed by the mercy of God and one whom God has decided to use, despite my sin. I have learned much from the difficult experience I've been through, and I have a much greater compassion now for all those who have been through or may go through similar experiences of loss."

## 8. How might I explain conflict or an involuntary termination to a search committee?

If a search committee asks you to explain conflict or involuntary termination at a previous parish, tell them the truth. But tell them this truth in a way that reassures them you will not give them any cause for concern in the future. Do remember, always, to speak well of your past employers—remember the search committee is weighing the future *only*. They will infer how you are going to speak and think about them from how you speak and think about past churches where you have been. You'll have to use your own words and your own thoughts, but you might want to make some statement similar to the following: "It was just one of those rare occurrences: similar to a marriage between two wonderful people, that inexplicably breaks up despite the best efforts of both parties. In such experiences, as in divorce, you know that it always takes two before you have an irreparable break. I've meditated long and hard on what I contributed to that, and I think as a result of God's help, I am a much more mature individual now. As to what that parish contributed to the breakup, I'd rather be a gentleman (or a lady) and respect their confidentiality."

## 9. How can I plan for a productive interview with the search committee?

A useful rule of thumb when face to face with a search committee is that you talk 50% of the time and you let/encourage them to talk 50% of the time. Further, that in answering *any* question they ask, you limit your answer to somewhere between twenty seconds and two minutes at a time (no more). When it's your turn to ask them questions, you will need to have the questions written out ahead of time. Generally speaking, you are going to be asking them whatever it is that *you will wish you had known after you accept the call.* To aid you in compiling the list, think of all the experiences you have had (or your clergy friends have had) that made them say, "If I'd known *that* I'd never have accepted this call." If necessary, get a group of your clergy friends together before your interview with that search committee and brainstorm what kinds of questions you need to ask. As for the order in which to put the questions during the interview, the general rule is: Ask first those questions that affect what you can give to them; ask last of all those questions which affect what they can give to you (like working conditions, days off, vacation time and—last, last of all—salary and perquisites).

### 10. What's the most appropriate way for clergy spouses to handle the search in this day and age?

If you are married, many search committees will view this as a chance to get two pastors for the price of one (whether or not your spouse is ordained). You *may* find a place where you are sure you could be happy and do a most effective work, *but* your spouse doesn't like the place at all, *or* the search committee doesn't like your spouse. (Your spouse, incidentally, should always be themself during the search process. I said this earlier, but I'll repeat it again: trying to remember some role to play will always backfire after you are settled in. The parish will feel "taken." Let them see who your spouse truly is as well as who you truly are. That way if they choose you, it will be a bargain based on honesty.) But suppose they don't like your spouse or your spouse doesn't like them? The hard truth here is that you probably should turn such a place down. There are other things you can do. (We're back to point #2, above.) You wouldn't accept that call, would you, if every time you set foot in the place, your right arm went into a paroxysm of pain? Why? Because God's calling is to your whole self, and if part of that self is in misery, the whole self will be in misery. So it is with your marriage: "The two shall become one." The call is to your whole self, and if you are married, that includes your spouse. All parts of you must accept the call, or none. That applies to dual-career couples also, where the issue is not the church but the town.

### 11. Should a candidate ask for a candid explanation of why he/she did not get a job?

If you meet with a search committee and decide you would really love to be called there, but they choose someone else, you have *the right* to gently inquire why you didn't get called. Equally, the search committee has *the right* not to answer that question. There is a body of secular law that is rapidly growing where massive awards have been made *against* employers and to would-be employees for discrimination or unlawful discharge. Many search committees therefore will be *extremely* reluc-

tant to answer your question at all candidly, lest you be gathering material for going to law. You can, to some extent, get around this by not
asking them why they didn't call you, but rather asking them for advice.
This way you're not probing the past, you're focusing on the future. The
question you can address to them without raising any legal specters is: "I
am continuing to search for a place where God can use my talents. Do
you, on the basis of your experience with me, have any advice for me as
to how I could better conduct myself in that search at the next parish
where I may interview? I'm particularly anxious to know if I have any
personal mannerisms or traits or ways of answering questions that are,
well, off-putting. I would be deeply grateful for any advice or feedback
you could give me." This is, incidentally, better done with a phone call
than in a letter so that their answer can remain verbal and "off the record."

## 12. What kind of contract should I ask for?

As to the matter of contracts, some parishes will give them, some simply
won't. The time to ask about that is only after they have actually called
you and you are still debating what to answer them. Any earlier raising
of the issue is presumptuous; any later raising of the issue is too late.
The purpose of a contract, if you can get one, is to protect you and them
from any misunderstanding or any unintentional amnesia, on either of
your parts, about things you care about in the verbal agreement you both
reached. A *good* contract (which you may *never* see in your entire
lifetime) would spell out *both* what you are offering them *and* what they
are offering you—in other words, both sides get protected. Of course,
the concept of "sides" is what is wrong with the whole concept of A
Contract to begin with. If you're dealing with a body whose words you
don't quite trust, that's something to think about *before* you accept the
call. On the other hand, vestries or executive committees do rotate, and a
contract is a nice way of reminding future incumbents what it was that
the previous incumbents committed them to.

## 13. I've been looking and looking, and I'm getting discouraged. What can I do now?

So long as you remain a priest (or other ordained person) and want to
work for the church, you are in the position essentially of going after One
Employer. The reason for this truism is that while on the surface of it

there are many different parishes and therefore many different places of opportunity, in actual fact there is also such a thing as a "parish culture" which infects and invades virtually all parishes across the board. Since you are trying to find employment from One Employer, you are very much like an engineer who is determined to work only for GE. If GE wants her (or him), great! But if not, the first thing you in your wisdom would counsel that person would be, "Don't restrict yourself to going after just one employer—even if there are many GE plants scattered across the country, they're still all GE. Broaden your plan." So too, you must advise yourself. If after all your best efforts to find employment within the church, you feel disappointed and depressed, you must face squarely the possibility that through this frustrating experience, God is at work—(yes I know you know that, but let me finish)—God is *using* that process *to call you outside the church* for your next chapter in your vocation to Him. Do look at this very hard and very seriously and very prayerfully. It's hard to remember this when you're going through the search process, but throughout your entire vocation, your ultimate transaction is with God and not with His church—or only incidentally with His church. He has found you pleasing in His sight. It helps to remember that on the days when the church does not.

CHAPTER II

# Build Your Search Around Your Giftedness

*by Arthur F. Miller, Jr.*

Issues of job search, job fit, and career direction are prematurely addressed until the person comes to an accurate and complete understanding of what the Bible calls his "ways" or mode-of-action. (Jeremiah 17:10; II Chronicles 6:30; I Kings 8:39; Job 34:11; Ezekiel 18:30; Proverbs 5:21) For if you study your history of personal achievement as we have since 1961 studied an average of 400-500 people each year, you will make a profound discovery: that you possess a mode-of-action, a distinct "way" of operating when you are at your most productive and most fulfilled. You have repeatedly used certain abilities; concentrated on certain subjects and objects; required certain structure, visibility, standards, outcome, and conditions; functioned in a certain relationship with others; and achieved a certain payoff of precious personal significance.

In other words, you possess and express a patterned uniqueness. Literally, you have been endowed with an intricate design of giftedness, and you desire to use those gifts in certain ways for certain purposes under certain circumstances.

## How to Discover Your Design

How do you discover your design? The best way is through your enjoyable achievement experiences—things you have done in any area of your life which you enjoyed doing and believe you did well. Formally, we call this process the System for Identifying Motivated Abilities (SIMA) and the end product a Motivational Pattern.*

*Described in detail in *The Truth About You* by Miller/Mattson, Ten Speed Press and *Finding a Job You Can Love* by Mattson/Miller, Thomas Nelson Publishers.

**Step One:  Recalling Those Special Times**

Take a day (yes, a day) and write out as many brief statements of your
enjoyable achievement experiences as you can remember.  Start as early
in your life as you can recall.  When you run out of thoughts, put it aside
and come back to it.

Do not introduce any measurement of what you recall other than:
(1) did I do it well? and (2) did I enjoy it or find it satisfying?  Whether it
would impress anybody else is irrelevant (unless impact on others is your
bag).  How you compare to a superstar is irrelevant (unless you are motivated to be better than others).  Some examples drawn from our files:

-- Fixed anything mechanical.
-- Helped my friend through a crisis.
-- Became accepted by the jocks and the eggheads and the tough
    kids.
-- Used to almost always win in Monopoly.
-- Read three books a week for two years.
-- Led an insurrection at the seminary.
-- Saved a girl from drowning.
-- Helped a family confront the death of a child.
-- Had a radio ministry for five years.
-- Made all my own clothes.
-- Nursed a cow back to health.
-- Became top altar boy.
-- Was the first black to break the barrier.
-- Built a church from scratch to 500 members.
-- Started a newsletter which increased support.

**Step Two:  Talking It Out**

Get a good friend who is patient, a good listener, and, ideally, can help
you come forward with the facts.  Use a tape recorder and start describ-
ing how you went about making and flying that seven-foot kite.  Start
with your earliest achievement and talk about:

-- How you got involved in the first place.
-- What you found satisfying about what you did.
-- The details of how you did what you did.

This is probably the key: the details of how you did what you did. Push yourself here. You probably have never explained to anyone, including yourself, how you raised the prize heifer, or resolved a schism in the church, or learned how to RAP in one month, or counseled a friend not to leave home.

This is an example of the kind of rich detail you should be generating when you describe your achievements:

> In Vietnam, assigned as Lieutenant, Company Supply Officer...felt I had the ability to understand these people...could understand what they wanted, what they liked. Most of the COs ignored these people. The guys felt close to me because they'd come in and talk to me. If a guy liked electricity, I led him to believe I was interested too. I'd ask him questions...make him feel I appreciated what he'd done. Each one of them had a specialty...they could fix anything, make anything. If they didn't like it, they were not going to do it. They'd help each other out...never had more than 6-7 guys, but they were on call 24 hours a day...had to let them always think they were doing the greatest, which they were as far as I was concerned...let them know they were appreciated. Guess that was the way I motivated them. If they wanted some recognition, I'd write them a letter and let the CO sign it. If they wanted to sit down and talk to me about their problem, I let them. Consequently they all worked for me...anything I wanted...amazed a CO more than once I suppose. The job itself didn't turn me on at all...just to see that I was able to get these people to improve was satisfying.

Is the point clear? You need to describe *detail*. Every time you say you did something—like "I conducted the first retreat," or "I did some research," or "I learned how to paint," or "I designed the program," or "I made my own garden"—describe *how* you went about doing it.

Place yourself back in the exact situation and describe how you went about it. Exhaust your recollection of the detail. Don't stop until you cannot remember anything else. Ask your friend to press you for more details about anything *you* have described.

What you do not do:
   -- Don't talk about your feelings—just talk about what you did.
   -- Don't stray from what *you* did and *how* you went about doing it.
   -- Don't just talk about experiences (I love to read), but identify

something you actively did (I love to read mysteries and figure
out who did it).
-- Don't talk generalities (I love preaching) but specifics (I love to
move people with my sermons on relationships).
-- Give examples which would illustrate what you mean or how you
functioned, i.e., how you got the idea, studied for the test, came
up with a strategy, acted the part.

**Step Three: Gathering Up the Pieces**

Having described in detail no less than a dozen enjoyable achievement
experiences, listen to the tape or, best, type up what you said. You
should have a minimum of fifteen double-spaced pages or an hour of
tape to listen to. Whether you listen to the tape or work from a typed
transcript, your goal is to identify any recurring themes or trends which
reveal the following kinds of information, i.e., the ingredients of your
Motivational Pattern.

1. What is the **Subject Matter** of your achievements?
   *(Look for 3-5 elements.)*

   -- Do you find people as a recurring theme? If so, are you dealing
   with individuals, groups, or both? Or perhaps you are interested
   in people as a society or culture?
   -- What about words or language?
   -- Or maybe details?
   -- What about concepts or principles or ideas?
   -- Are math or numbers in your material?
   -- Do you find physical or mechanical or material things?
   -- Are you turned on by visual or sensory items like color or texture
   or shapes or rhythm?
   -- Do you find machinery or equipment?
   -- What about physical or biological sciences?

Do *not* regard this list as exhaustive. Use it to stimulate your effort.

2. What **Abilities** did you repeatedly use?
   *(Look for 6-9 elements.)*

Examine your achievements to determine what you were doing with the subject matter you have already identified. Say it was the game of tennis, and among other similar manifestations you have identified (gardening, skiing, weight lifting), you conclude physical/manual things are a preferred subject matter. Now the question confronting you is, with what abilities did you work your magic on the sport of tennis?

Well, first of all, you learned how to play tennis by taking a racquet and hitting a ball against a wall. Then you got someone to hit balls to you over a net while you tried different shots. Then you actually played the game with a friend who was good at it and helped you experiment with different ways of serving and striking the ball.

*(So we pick up the fact that you apparently learn by doing and experimenting.)*

During this period, you began to attend some local tennis matches where you spent hours watching the better players. When you were impressed by particular players, you went to see them after the game and asked questions.

*(Now we've identified some observational skills and an ability to probe or interview to ascertain data or knowledge of significance.)*

As you described the next phase, you talked about identifying the strengths and weaknesses of people you were scheduled to play in the local tournament. Then you described how you would develop a strategy for exploiting what you had observed.

*(Here you manifested further observing skills but also an evaluating and strategizing ability.)*

When you described an actual match you played, you stressed how you psyched out your opponent not only by refusing to come to the net where she was strong, but also by numerous little tricks which would slow down her fast game or cause minor irritations.

*(Here we see more evaluating and strategizing but also some influencing by subtly manipulating the other person.)*

3. What **Circumstances** frequently recur in your achievements?
   *(Look for 3-6 elements.)*

An important aspect of your Motivational Pattern emerges in particular elements of a situation which, if absent, would make it of less or no motivating value. Because the presence or absence of these elements can be crucial in managing your career, you need to sift through your achievements to identify the presence of particular circumstances of motivating value to you.

What triggers your achievements?
- -- a problem to solve
- -- needs to be met
- -- a confronting test or challenge
- -- a cause to be served
- -- head-to-head competition
- -- a crisis

Do your achievements reveal a need for definition/structure?
- -- Don't fence me in—little if any structure.
- -- I like to know the rules of the road.
- -- I need a script.
- -- I need to know what the boss wants.
- -- I want a goal and a structure within which to operate.

Is a desire for recognition revealed in your achievements?
- -- I have to be seen—personal credit is critical.
- -- Audiences are frequently present in my achievements.
- -- Notoriety or reputation comes through as important.
- -- I'm a behind-the-scenes support person, but I like people to know I'm back there.

Do particular working conditions surface in your achievements?
- -- Pressure is always a part of my achievements.
- -- Plenty of learning time is critical.
- -- I really need deadlines.
- -- Having to think on my feet is highly motivating.
- -- I'm mostly outdoors in my achievements.

Is certainty of result part of your achievements?
- -- I need a standard.
- -- A finished product is what I seek.
- -- My work has to be used by someone.

-- I've got to know the objective for my efforts.
-- I've got to make or break previous results or there's no point.

4. How do your achievements describe your **Relationship** with others?
   *(Look for 1-2 elements.)*

   -- Do you function as a *contributor* where you personally
      accomplish something and do not require others to take action?
   -- Do your achievements reveal you want to function as an
      *influencer* where you want to cause others to take action, but
      you do not want continuing or overall responsibility for
      managing others?
   -- Do you want to use others, as a *manager,* to accomplish an end
      and seek overall responsibility over others?
   -- Are you a *leader*, inspiring others to follow you though you may
      have no interest in managing them?

5. What **Motivational Payoff** (what you want out of life) do your
achievements show?
   *(Look for 1 element.)*

There is one consistent payoff in all of your achievement experiences. If
you can understand that outcome, even generally, you will understand
much about why you move the way you do in life. The following are
summaries of such motivational payoffs. Choose one.

   -- You want to stand out over others (excel, be different, be key).
   -- You want to exercise dominion or power (be in charge, overcome,
      master, acquire).
   -- You want to impact on a person, object, situation (improve it,
      extract potential, gain response).
   -- You delight in a process by itself (develop, build, realize concept).
   -- You respond to a defined challenge (fulfill requirements, meet the
      text, reach the objective).

**Verification Process**

The foregoing represents some of the elements of your strengths that I
call your Motivational Pattern. If you or your friend-assistant has
questions about any conclusion reached, you can verify that conclusion

by gathering evidence from your achievements which clearly reveals its presence.

### Sample Motivational Pattern

When you finish identifying your pattern, it should look something like this:

What Subject Matter is worked with or through?
    -- structural objects
    -- concepts and principles
    -- people (groups)
    -- systems

What Motivated Abilities are used?
    -- reading and studying
    -- visualizing
    -- evaluating
    -- organizing
    -- developing
    -- persuading
    -- doing, implementing

What Circumstances are involved?
    -- from scratch, from nothing
    -- visibility
    -- goals, objectives
    -- stress, pressure

What Operating Relationships are established with others?
    -- influencer

What is the one Motivational Payoff?
    -- meeting a defined challenge

### The Ideal Job

One of the best things you do with your Motivational Pattern is to use it to construct an ideal job objective. The first thing to do is examine what you have to give to a church, which is the same thing, understood properly, as what you want out of life. To move from your Motivational Pattern to a fruitful career direction, it is important that the pattern be read, understood, and used as an integral system of strengths and motivations. Do not make the mistake of extracting one or another quality and saying it is universally typical of you. Only when integrated with all the other parts of the pattern can one part properly be understood. However you want to look at at, the way you can outline your ideal job is to synthesize the elements of your Motivational Pattern into a single statement. There are many ways of pulling those pieces together, but here is one approach you can use.

**A job working with**...*(insert your Subject Matter—e.g., people, ideas, numbers, structural things, etc.)*

**The conditions of the work**...*(insert your Circumstances—e.g., project oriented, require operating under stress, allow freedom of movement, etc.).*

**And where I can operate**...*(insert your Way of Operating with others—e.g., in a team, in a defined role, in a leadership capacity, etc.).*

**Using my motivated abilities to**...*(insert your Motivated Abilities— e.g., investigate for the facts, analyze their significance, improvise a solution, organize others involved, oversee the implementation, etc.)*

**And which leads to**...*(insert your one Motivational Payoff—e.g., a finished product, chance for advancement, greater responsibility, recognition for my contribution, etc.)*

In filling out this format, use whatever filler words make it flow and communicate your strengths in a clear, easily-understood manner. In its almost finished form, it should look like the following:

### Ideal Church

A job as pastor of a small- to medium-sized church in a suburban area, working with a mix of ages, races, income, education, biblical literacy, and spiritual maturity. Openness of the congregation to new concepts, changing values, and community needs and expansion of mission dollars would be important. I want freedom to spend time on noncongregational projects and to delegate poor fit areas to others. Opportunity as an authority to preach on contemporary issues, develop and lead a network of small home groups focused on social action, facilitate work project discussion among teenagers in mutually supportive teams...which will lead to changed attitudes and lives.

Remember that we are starting with a description of your ideal job. It is unlikely that you will find a church with every element of your pattern employed in this way. However, as a basis of comparison, it is good to have a concise statement of what you are shooting for, even if it is idealized somewhat. Taking the time to synthesize the elements of your Motivational Pattern in this way will give you a compact, more easily-understood way of remembering your MAP, a goal to aim at in your planning, and a means of evaluating a particular job fit.

Having done the preceding homework, you next need to understand the significance of your design to get at the many career/job/role questions you have. To start out, you need to realize that effectively, your design is you. Since your acceptance of that premise is so critical to effective management of your career, I'm going to spell out what we have observed as demonstrable characteristics of this patterned uniqueness. Because so much in the modern age promises self-transcendence, it is important you not get seduced into the notion of becoming what others (or you yourself) need or want you to become. Even if you can simulate a different person, what you produce is ersatz fruit, and what you inherit is destructive stress. Embrace the early Hellenic and Greek dual aphorisms "Know thyself." and "Become what you are." or far better yet, embrace biblical truths: "For we are God's handiwork, created in Christ Jesus, to perform the good deeds for which we were designed." (Ephesians 2:1) To take in the notion that we each are designed, let's look at the nature of motivational patterns.

## Early Emergence and Consistency of Motivational Patterns

Most people recall an achievement activity from as early as five or six years old, some can remember back to age three or four, and a few people describe experiences that occurred even earlier. At whatever age achievement activities are recalled as beginning, a behavior pattern is well fleshed out by the middle teens. Your Motivational Pattern matures through the demands of increasingly complex achievement activities as you grow, but its essence remains consistent.

*For example:*
> You were good at solving puzzles when you were five.
> Not even in kindergarten were you willing to follow the procedures.

## Patterns Are Irrepressible

You continuously attempt to exercise your Motivational Pattern in spite of your situation. The reality you perceive is shaped by the pattern; it affects how you approach your work. When the motivational value of a task has been exhausted, you will seek a new arena. You can slump into despondency if circumstances collude to prevent your pattern's expression over a long period of time. You will attempt to order any situation to receive personal satisfaction. You will resist conflicting demands and may distort conventional expectations when they do not align with your intentions.

*For example:*
> You keep evangelizing the saved.
> Your keep urging people to go over the next hill.

## Patterns Appear Innate

A person comes into the world with the seeds of a unique Motivational Pattern present and functioning. Our opinion about this is based on many observations that refute the influence on behavior credited to environmental factors. We have found no correlation between motivational patterns and the environment in which an individual was raised. For example, siblings raised by parents in the same environment turn out wonderfully unique. People who participated in similar activities while growing up have diverse behavior patterns as adults. Besides, we have never encountered a client who acquired a gift not possessed since childhood.

*For example:*
> Wherever you go, people remark about your quickness of mind.
> You're the only sibling who doesn't worry about money.

## The Duality of Behavior

When involved in an activity that does not motivate you, behavior is different from that displayed when you are doing something that has motivating value. The difference occurs because motivated behavior reflects your will and giftedness and unmotivated behavior does not. Unmotivated behavior is caused by external necessities and social forces: "I ought to do this though I don't want to" or "my church would be disappointed if I didn't do this" are indicative of behavior grounded outside the Motivational Pattern.

*For example:*
> Whenever you try to counsel you get very stressed.
> You can teach all day without getting tired.

## Patterns Reveal Giftedness

People are naturally good at the abilities, subject matter, circumstances, and relationships described in the Motivational Pattern. They were good, even as children, at working with numbers, at getting people organized, at noticing detail, at exerting leadership over others, at seeing beyond the obvious, at anticipating problems, at fantasizing, at throwing a ball, at playing a role. When you consult those close to you, you will find that you are known and perceived as gifted in those behaviors captured in the Motivational Pattern.

*For example:*
> You really are brilliant at clarifying complex theology.
> You are a klutz when you visit the sick.

## Emotions Are Sensitized and Colored by Patterns

Strong emotional reactions can often be traced to your Motivational Pattern. Joy and a sense of meaning are by-products of achievement activities. Intimidation and anxiety frequently occur when you are tested in areas that fall outside your strengths. You may be nervous if asked to give an offhand report when your normal approach is methodical and comprehensive. Anger and defensiveness can stem from remarks or actions that appear to attack motivational treasures.

*For example:*
> Systematic theology comforts your soul.
> Exercise of charismatic spiritual gifts makes you nervous.

**Your Mind Functions in Accordance with Your Pattern**

Your Motivational Pattern affects how you learn; what subjects you
learn; why you learn; whether you learn in a team setting or alone or in a
team setting after independently acquiring background knowledge.

*For example:*
Quiet reading time in preparation for your sermons is an absolute.
Current happenings in the congregation constitute your sermon
gristmill.

**Performance Is Dominated by Patterns**

The influence of your Motivational Pattern continues long after the
learning process and determines how you perceive a role should be per-
formed. You will not perform according to a job description unless it
matches your Motivational Pattern. Regardless of what the church thinks
is needed, a pastor motivated to innovate will try to innovate; one motivated to control will set up controls; one motivated to overcome problems will look for and find problems; a pastor motivated to build relationships will do so.

*For example:*
But he has alienated half the congregation with his views.
I don't know why she can't see that the kids need help.

**Motivational Patterns Characterize Social Behavior**

Your Motivational Pattern is reflected in all areas of your life. Not only
is it revealed in the way a person approaches tasks, it can be seen at work
in aspects of one's social life that, at first, appear to be merely a matter of
personal taste or style. For example, in conversation, the pastor motivated to impress others relives his trip to a war-torn country. A pastor
motivated to meet needs encourages a parishioner to reveal a current
difficulty, then offers counsel. A pastor motivated to prevail intuitively
moves toward a weakness revealed in another's position, whereas a pastor motivated to interact one-on-one makes an intense conversationalist.
Advocates are known for sermonizing while performers are known for
their liveliness and wit.

The formation and outcome of personal relationships is also highly dependent on an individual's Motivational Pattern. Some pastors are motivated to cultivate close relationships, and their parishioners consider them to play an important role in their life. Pastors who attempt to shape others often have a history of transient relationships with problem people or younger, inexperienced individuals. Similarly, motivational elements reflecting a desire for filling needs, eliteness, controlling situations, exploiting potential, uniqueness, team membership, and a chance to demonstrate personal expertise all find their expression in the kind and length of relationships a pastor forms.

Conflict between pastor and lay leader or pastor and parishioner frequently can be traced to their motivational patterns. Understanding the other's Motivational Pattern often leads the way to resolution. Examples can be found in every kind of relationship: a take-charge pastor with independent lay leaders; an individualist pastor married to a team member husband; a counselor who wants to teach, advising a client who wants to learn on his own; a hands-on pastor of a yuppie congregation; a pastor who desires a supportive congregation working for one which is gifted at criticism and murmuring; a pastor motivated to win negotiating with a committee motivated to prevail; the pastor who attempts to meet all the requirements working with a lay leader motivated to innovate.

## Motivational Patterns Are Amoral But Value Prone

A person can use his or her Motivational Pattern either constructively or destructively. Knowledge of patterns has not been helpful for predicting actions that involve issues of integrity, loyalty, or honesty. A thief can be gifted, a genius can purvey drugs.

> The rebellious were given gifts so the Lord God might dwell among them.
>
> > (Psalms 68:18)

Having said this, we must also add that many pastors take a particular theological, social, or moral stance because it engages their motivational patterns. They may favor infant baptism, hierarchical organization, relational theology, local congregational autonomy, reconstructionism, local evangelism, inerrancy of Scripture, etc., because of their motivational predisposition.

**Predestination Run Amuck?**

If I haven't exhausted you with the preceding description of some important dynamics of motivational patterns, you may have been muttering about predestination. Admittedly, our observations seem to support the philosophy of determinism. However, human actions are not inevitable because each of us is driven by a pattern. Humans are capable of making genuine decisions. You should not believe all your decisions are inevitable. You decide certain things should happen, and they wouldn't happen unless you made that decision. The pattern describes how you decide and how you act once you decide. So, while we recognize the human ability to make decisions, we also recognize the pattern's influence on our decision-making processes and actions.

Stating that you are your pattern is helpful to clarify that your pattern is not something you possess. But do not conclude that your Motivational Pattern describes your entire personality. We know that patterns are the core of being an individual; but the human personality is extremely complex, and we do not claim that patterns can answer all the questions you have about yourself. Patterns have little to say about character and whether you are honest or loyal or just. But understanding the power of your Motivational Pattern will provide you with the means to make some sound career decisions and enhance your effectiveness and the ministry of the church.

## The Payoff

If you will go through the effort of really understanding your Motivational Pattern, almost all the questions confronting you about your current role, making a decision to move on, or accepting/rejecting a particular call will be readily answered.

First, if you have never done so, now would be a good time to answer the foundational question of whether or not you should be in the ministry of a Protestant church. If you have identified major elements of your giftedness, the answer is usually clear.

> -- Am I motivated to get involved with people?
> -- Am I motivated to work one-on-one?
> -- Am I motivated to work with groups?
> -- Am I motivated to meet needs?
> -- Am I motivated to preach?

-- Am I motivated to cause learning?
-- Am I motivated to enable the development of others?
-- Am I motivated to counsel others?

If the answers to those questions are uniformly "no," then the parish ministry is obviously not your calling. To the extent you come up with more "no" than "yes" answers, you should be concerned about suitability. It is one thing to be enamored of preaching and/or teaching, but if you honestly do not like to get involved with people, you must be one of two or more pastors, one of whom could fill that void.

Assuming suitability, refer to your ideal church statement we earlier suggested you prepare to guide you in your search. If you aren't able to work up such a recipe, try identifying with one or two of the following:

**The Pastor as Star**
Performance is focused on personal performance.

**The Pastor as Master**
Performance is focused on gaining and maintaining control or dominion over situations, people, knowledge, institutions.

**The Pastor as Shepherd**
Performance is focused on the congregation and the facilities: causing response, fixing, extracting, improving, impacting.

**The Pastor as Builder**
Performance is focused on the process of developing and advancing the buildings, programs, and competencies.

**The Pastor as Responder**
Performance is focused on meeting needs, fulfilling requirements, and satisfying expectations.

If you know clearly what your design says about your giftedness and motivational outcome or payoff, the job search becomes a matter of finding a church that wants what you have and want to give. You look for a church that needs and, ideally, wants your mix of gifts.

To aid in this process, begin to put more meat on the bones of your Motivational Pattern. If I am motivated to work with others in some way, are the "others":

-- spiritual neophytes?
-- people with problems?
-- seeking people?
-- stimulating people?
-- uneducated people?

Again regarding a congregation, am I motivated:

-- to keep them in the church?
-- to take them deeper into their spiritual life?
-- to knock their socks off?
-- to make their numbers grow?
-- to introduce them to the new and unique?
-- to cause an emotional response?
-- to straighten them out?
-- to lead them in liturgical ceremony?
-- to solve their problems?
-- to meet their expectations?
-- to join with them in their lives and struggles?

Keep probing your own giftedness and motivation so you will more readily recognize a likely match or mismatch when you see it. Do your achievements reveal that you want to:

-- start a church from nothing?
-- build a church at a growing stage?
-- run an established church?
-- turn around a mature troubled church?

Review your achievements and rehearse with yourself the kinds of outcomes you expect from your ministry:

-- deepened relationship with God?
-- quantitative results?
-- problems solved?
-- new programs developed?
-- improvement in knowledge?
-- impact on quality of lives/caring?

Look carefully at how you need to be "managed" to feel turned-on and fully engaged:

-- hands-off?
-- hands-on?
-- involved but collaborative?
-- clearly in charge?

If you know the issues, environment, attitudes necessary for you to prosper, you won't get misled by all the side roads pursued by most search committees and candidates. Questions about handling yourself in a job search to assure an ultimate match can be dealt with best by knowing and expressing who you are and probing what responding need/situation would accommodate what you have to give. For example, if you want to be the "expert," you would go hard at determining the background and spiritual/biblical sophistication of the congregation. Or, if you thrived under a more interactive, participative climate, you would probe to ascertain the nature of educational efforts; previous minister's style and how it went over; educational and vocational background of the congregation.

Those are two simple examples, but they can perhaps help you understand how your job search should revolve around your design if you are to find and win a suitable match. Issues of your being a performer; loving concepts, research, and exegesis; helping the needy; winning souls; building a family and playing father or mother; or crusading for or against something should guide your investigation into the potential for its prospering.

One practical way of matching you and the church is to put your strengths down the left hand side of a page and get enough information to know (1) whether that particular strength would be used and (2) whether the church's expectations draw on motivated competencies you don't possess. As a minimum, your self-knowledge gives you a check list of items to be explored.

Always remember, you are God's idea and design. Your job is to find the church that needs what you have been given to give.

If you know what is imperative to you, concentrate your inquiry of the church and the presentation of who you are around who you are and what you need to bless the people of that church.

# CHAPTER III

# The Job Search: What Are My Choices?

*by Russell C. Ayers*

## Section A: Identifying Choices amidst the Anxiety of the Job Search

Congregational profiles, personal profiles, resumes, computer matching, job descriptions, interviews, raiding parties from congregations looking for a new pastor, guest sermons for calling committees, tapes of sermons in the mail, waiting for a telephone call or a letter about making the cut... Such stress! Such grief! Such anxiety!

Some of us handle it better than others. There are those among us who are pastors, priests, and rabbis who seem to have the greatest good fortune when it comes to making a good lateral or upward career move. For a few lucky ones, a call to a new parish comes out of the blue and it turns out to be nearly perfect. And there are others who make the smallest effort in exploring new pastorates, and they are offered not one but two or three positions.

Even though many of us know or are aware of persons with such good fortune, there aren't really so many of them as it might seem. Out of hundreds of career moves I have witnessed, such occurrences seem to be precious few. I have, in fact, known or heard of only ten or twenty changes in pastorates where everything went easily and smoothly.

Something far more difficult seems to happen for clergy facing the inevitable change in pastorates. Clergy often experience significant stress when making a pastoral or career change even if the move goes fairly well. Such changes are often full of confusion, mixed emotions, and a lot of anguish.

## Job Search Anxiety Seems to Be Universal

Robert Oden, Headmaster of the Hotchkiss School, said in an address at the Smithsonian Institution in April, 1990: "Something in our culture, perhaps from Puritanism, suggests that each individual has a sense of a God-given vocation, a unique role to fill, without a knowledge of which a state of near non-being exists."[1] He went on to say that the anxiety associated with seeking and finding one's vocation is higher in America than anywhere else in the world. Status in our community and in our peer groups is often based on what one's job is. Basic social exchanges include the questions, "What do you do?" or "What are you going to do?" If we can't answer these questions for ourselves, let alone for others, anxiety is usually the result.

**The Day Comes**

For most clergy, the day comes when it is apparent that job satisfaction and fulfillment are not going to be found in the present work situation. Thoughts of seeking a new position come into consciousness. Concerns and conflicts emerge: "I don't like this job." "I think I'm going to lose this job." "What else can I do?" "Can I do anything else?" Associated with these questions are feelings of vulnerability and anxiety. One can lose touch with a sense of self and experience diminished self-worth and feelings of failure as one's position as pastor either suddenly or slowly comes into doubt. "It wasn't supposed to be like this."

By the time a person gets to the point of asking these questions, very often he or she has lost touch with how and why he or she reached this point. It can be most instructive to identify the sources of anxiety about one's present work. Sometimes the focusing process helps us discover options or identify reasons for dissatisfaction that hadn't been considered previously. You really need to know why you are feeling dissatisfied and anxious in your present situation in order to either stay or move on.

There are a variety of situations and conditions which cause us to pursue the idea of a change of pastorate. For purposes of this chapter we will look at the professional situations and then at personal situations which prompt us to think about moving.

## Reasons for Moving On

### Professional Situations and Conditions

1. Underemployment and the attendant boredom which follows is one such experience. Clergy sometimes find themselves in positions for which they are *over qualified and mismatched* in terms of ministry needs

and the energy they have to give to their ministry. One's experience, continuing education, and personal growth can contribute to developing skills and interests which are more suited to a different type, style, or size congregation. The result can range from simple frustration to a sense of being trapped and anxious. These negative energies can even keep us from exploring ways to apply new skills in our present work situation until a more substantial change is accomplished.

2. Getting buried in the culture of a congregation can lead to a loss of intentionality and a loss of identity as pastor or priest. "Getting buried in a culture" refers to a condition where a cleric over-identifies with the needs and issues of the people and institution and becomes immersed in those needs in an unhealthy way, all under the guise of ministry. Lacking the skills for maintaining a differentiated role as pastor and leader can lead to patterns of relating to the congregation which are not easily changed. Such lack of differentiation can lead to a loss of personal autonomy which might then prompt a man or woman to consider going someplace for a fresh start to recover a sense of self.

3. Unresolved struggles and special challenges in the parish or community may provide the setting for the desire for a change. When clergy try and try to resolve struggles and challenges with no apparent positive or measurable result, they are likely to become demoralized. When one has tried everything one could think of and made use of every resource imaginable, including consultants and "experts," a cleric may begin to feel himself or herself to be entirely ineffectual if not a failure. The reaction in this kind of situation usually generates a desire for flight and escape, and a desire to find a new challenge somewhere else that is more realistic and productive.

4. Discouragement which comes about as a result of prolonged conflict is easily one of the chief reasons any pastor will think about moving to a new place. Conflict and stress reduce self-esteem and a sense of worth in the performance of most of one's duties. The corrosive nature of some parishes' lifestyles saps one's energy, and a defensive survival posture is all that is available. General discouragement can lead to the more serious state of burnout.

5. Another condition that I would characterize as "role performance anxiety" deserves attention. Work becomes a series of events and

occurrences that you don't understand. The misunderstanding is rooted either in what is being communicated by others or in confusion about what you believe and or feel for yourself. You may not be sure what the problem is or what you ought to do.

A sorting out process is needed—through extended conversations with sensitive and insightful colleagues, through getting away from the environment long enough to develop perspective, or through entering therapy.

There are certainly other professional situations that prompt clergy to consider moving to a new pastorate, and much more could be said about those I have listed. It is *usual* for clergy to have these experiences. The more we know about them, the better equipped we will be to deal with them constructively, including making a move to a new congregation or parish when appropriate.

**Reasons for Moving On:  Personal Needs and Situations**

Some of the items we will call "personal" have very close connections to those factors which we call "professional," but they are slightly different. Following are personal responses or ways of coping to which clergy resort when they find themselves in difficult and corrosive situations. These responses can inhibit a pastor from facing the issues surrounding the need for a change.

*The Discouragement Factor*

So many conditions and experiences can cause discouragement! Sometimes clergy believe that this in itself is a sign of failure or unworthiness and as a result tend not to look into the reasons for their discouragement.

1. Negative Job-Search History
If you previously experienced a particularly difficult move from one pastorate to another, that might underlie your resistance to deal with the issues of whether to stay where you are or try to secure a new position. A sense of pain and anguish from previous job searches can be an inhibition to jumping into the fray of being a candidate again. If it was terribly hard to find your present position and you were hopeful that this would be a good fit, how much harder will this search be? Underlying a sense of being stuck may be the conviction that you chose poorly last time, so you may be thinking you aren't very good at this and it could happen again.

## 2. Exhaustion and Fatigue

Sometimes there is simply a bewildering array of evidence that being a leader of a religious body, whether it's a congregation or institution, is one of the most difficult roles in society today. It is demanding and stressful. Many clergy work an unreasonable number of hours on a regular basis. Some seem to reap little reward for all the effort. In some degree that's the nature of what it means to be pastor or priest. The resulting fatigue from just doing one's job results in little energy or even desire to expend the effort necessary for finding a new position. There is great irony in the lack of spiritual and psychic reward for spiritual leadership!

## 3. Hiding

There are a number of studies indicating some significant difference in the belief systems of pastors and congregations. Being more liberal or more conservative than the congregation you serve requires that you keep your opinions to yourself at important times. Awareness of such differences often surfaces in the midst of planning programs for religious education, evangelism, outreach, and stewardship (including fundraising). The debates about the entry and affiliation rites of a particular religious community are times when the difference between the pastor's views and the congregation's will be most noticeable. When differences of this sort are only generally sensed and not faced consciously clergy will often find ways to avoid conflict which serve to cover up the lack of fit between the congregation and the pastor.

For all intents and purposes we can call this "hiding." Sometimes you may think of yourself as a secret agent, a "deceiver yet true" as in the title of one of Kierkegaard's sermons. This may involve subtly influencing and moving the congregation by using sermons, programs, and symbols which are closer to your ideology/theology than theirs. All of this is exhausting. To live with such a perceived difference tends to generate a cynicism that keeps one from entering in and belonging and from being the leader of the community. Such cynicism may be projected onto congregations in general and affect your perspective as you wonder whether it will be any better anywhere else.

## 4. Failure

"It has always been clear that there was a challenge in this congregation. I felt really charged up during the first year or so. I didn't know exactly what was needed but I had high hopes and a lot of energy. We tried one thing after another. We may even have asked outsiders for help. I was the leader. Whatever is needed in this place, it hasn't happened yet. I thought I would be able to pull it off. I didn't rise to the occasion as I thought I could and would. For a while I thought it would be enough to survive, but that has given way to a need to escape. I am no longer safe. So I had better stay where I am and avoid further risk."

A sense of being a failure usually is attended with a large amount of stress, pressure, and probably anxiety as well. It's appropriate to try to assess just how much pressure you are living with. The following is a checklist of anxiety-producing circumstances or conditions which you may be experiencing right now:

> self-doubt, low self-esteem
> others' criticism
> significant conflict with individuals or with boards, trustees, or
>   groups of people
> personal financial crisis
> inappropriate use of alcohol or other stimulants or depressants
> crises in personal relationships—with your spouse or other family
>   members
> fatigue, exhaustion
> hiding
> perceiving yourself to be a victim
> feelings of powerlessness
> cynicism
> sense of failure

If you find that these words describe what you are experiencing then you need to take some positive steps on your own behalf. This may include getting some skilled help. Take a look at this next item to see if it describes anything you are experiencing.

## 5. Victim Mentality

Have you adopted the attitudes and role of the victim? Remember, victims are, by definition, powerless. Victims have to be rescued by someone from the outside or by a miraculous change in the behavior of the persecutors and in those whose inadequate response brought us to this predicament. Blaming others is evidence of falling into the trap of thinking you are a victim.

Even though clergy *are* sometimes victimized by dysfunctional systems and malicious individuals, it is important to your present welfare and future that you do not adopt the emotional posture of victim. Debilitation of spirit and mind follow difficulty all the more surely when you wait for someone to fix your life for you.

Professional reasons? Personal reasons? In the middle of a fifty to eighty hour week with the phone ringing, people dying, babies being born, and a trip to the grocery store already a day overdue, it's pretty hard to tell the difference between one kind of stress or anxiety and another kind. (To top it all off, there are even more.) It is an important exercise, however, to know and sort through the sources of the stress. This makes it possible to get a handle on them and to do something about them.

### Reasons for Anxiety That Include Both Professional and Personal Aspects

There are at least three factors that can be part of the struggle pastors experience when considering a move. The first is money and compensation, the second has to do with the large numbers of clergy looking for a limited number of positions, and the third has to do with age and the increasing difficulty of placing clergy who are in their fifties and sixties.

### 1. Money and Compensation

You and your family need more money. Can you get enough of an increase in cash salary to make the move worthwhile or should you stay in the same place with the security of your present paycheck? Even though there are sufficient reasons to seek a change, you might be tempted to bargain with yourself over the relative emotional and professional costs as compared to the financial security of staying where you are.

Combined with other resistances and factors discouraging you from seeking a change, the practical realities of what it costs to maintain a household, raise a family, and enjoy a degree of comfort constitute a strong set of reasons to avoid seeking a new pastorate. These considerations seem tempting and powerful in a declining economy, especially if economic conditions make present and future increases in compensation less likely.

"So what do I do with this anxiety over money? Do I stay put? Shall I go for it?" The temptation is to treat the question as an entirely economic one. Indeed, in certain circumstances you, with your family, will make an economic decision in order to meet known and pressing needs. In other circumstances you will want to renew your sense of call and assess the fit of your skills, interests, and competencies with the type of work you are able to do where you are. When the fit is good and the reward is otherwise great, you may find it more than tolerable to sacrifice the possibility of greater income for the satisfaction of the ministry you have.

### 2. The Number of Available Positions

The number of available positions in your denomination relative to the number of applicants or candidates seeking them may cause you to think there is little likelihood of a successful search and call process. In several denominations there is an apparent surplus of clergy. Increased enrollments in seminaries and a greater number of persons being ordained adds to the surplus clergy phenomenon. This is more true for the more desirable urban/metropolitan or suburban congregations and parishes which are relatively more affluent than rural, rural-suburban, or inner city churches.

Faced with these statistics, you may be tempted to think that your effort to find a satisfactory new position will be unsuccessful. You easily forget that many hundreds of calls will be extended in the year to come after the usual candidating processes are conducted. There are probably additional reasons why you would latch on to this rationale to stay where you are. If, in fact, you are demoralized and discouraged, your diminished sense of worth may be telling you that you will not compare favorably with others with whom you would compete for the available positions. It is essential that you get yourself in shape spiritually and emotionally to move with confidence and high expectation that God intends to use you in a ministry setting which will be a good match and fit for your motivated skills, competencies, and interests. There is a place where God needs you to be. Don't forget to trust the work of the Holy Spirit.

### 3. Your Age

Is it harder to make a good move when you are over fifty? The answer is "yes" and, also, "it depends." There is indeed a continuing preference for men and women in their twenties, thirties, and early forties to fill leadership positions in all areas of our society. This preference is strong in many congregations, especially if their culture and tradition concerning the call process requires a person of a certain age.

If a cleric believes he or she is not desirable or is in fact less able to perform the tasks of parish ministry, then this belief will be picked up by most of the people who will consider him or her in the candidating process. This attitude is an invitation to "discount" your application, and it sends the message that you are an unlikely prospect to be pastor of that congregation.

Is there anything that can overcome the age barrier or the resistance in a congregation to call someone who is fifty or sixty? It isn't guaranteed, but optimism, a straightforward presentation of yourself and your vision for ministry in the congregation where you are applying for consideration, and healthy self-respect go a long way toward making you a leading candidate.

There are many members and leaders of congregations who are ready for the maturity and breadth of experience that come with age. If you can keep the focus on the needs and hopes and dreams of the calling committee and congregation, you are more likely to be perceived as a prime candidate. Remember that younger men and women are not necessarily any more capable for the tasks of ministry than you are because of their age. If you believe that you are truly suited for the position, make the best possible case for yourself you can!

## Inadequate Coping with Job Anxiety and Frustration Usually Comes from Not Understanding What's Going On

Each of us imagines that we will make appropriate responses when we are experiencing difficulty. Sometimes we hear accounts of colleagues and other professionals whose careers have gone askew, and we think that we would never allow our own circumstances to come to such a state. It is humbling and discouraging to realize that we are "one of them." Here are some of the effects of anxiety and frustration on life and work.

Some ways of coping with conflicted feelings about one's present position or future prospects include occasional impulsive behavior, such as jumping into new responsibilities or activities for which there is little or no time and energy, or entering into a degree program or some other learning activity which serves to provide diversion *and* a good reason not to change one's present situation. Another impulsive reaction is to foster inappropriate relationships and perhaps misbehave.

Withdrawal and creating a world of isolation also are evidence of inadequate coping. All of these kinds of actions can be an anxious stab at trying to get some relief from the growing confusion, ennui, or discouragement about the present work situation.

## Moving to a New Mindset, Organizing Resources (Yours and Others) So You Can Do a Good Job of Finding a New Job

### Approaching the Search with Positive Attitudes

Let's begin with a look at some of the *attitudes* with which clergy may approach a job search. When they are positive, we lead with high expectations and confidence that we have skills and competencies, energy, and good will to offer to a congregation which also has high hopes and a vision of the future.

1. Maybe it's time to have a little talk with yourself

If anxiety and discouragement have held the high ground in your life for a while it may be that there is need for a new frame of mind and positive action. You know that this state of ambiguity and confusion isn't where you ought to be, but where and how do you begin to take steps to change these attitudes?

A place to begin is to inventory your own thinking. Ask yourself: What am I telling myself right now? What do I go to bed thinking? What do I wake up thinking? Am I stuck with the same attitudes and thoughts as yesterday and last week and last month? Since I tend to think and do what I rehearse, what script am I using to live out my life these days? Having asked these questions, you will want to remember that what you fantasize has a tremendous effect on what you feel, think, and do. If you fantasize defeat you will likely set up defeat; if you fantasize new possibilities then you will be more prepared for constructive steps and changes. Someone has said, "It's foolish not to win in our fantasies."

2. Talking with others

Resist the temptation to go it alone. One of the cardinal sins of clergy seems to be the lone-ranger syndrome in which men and women in ministry keep their most powerful thoughts and feelings to themselves, especially their pain and confusion. Consider whom you can speak to in candor. What limitations, if any, are there in your ability to be candid with each of these persons?  Do you need to look outside the congregation or outside the group of local clergy for some good reason?  In general, the group to whom you confide career doubts and anxieties and especially notions of leaving the ministry setting you are now in ought not to include local parishioners.  If you aren't comfortable taking clergy you know into your confidence, then pay someone, such as a pastoral counselor or therapist, to listen to you.

Talk to trustworthy persons who can verify your assessment of where you are, how you're doing, and what resources you have to use in the work of changing pastorates.

Find positive people and stay with them:  talk to people who believe in you.  Find a counselor who will contract with you for a supportive relationship for the duration of the sorting out process.  Find a positive program like Dick Bolles' annual two-week seminar[2] or Bart Lloyd's Life/Work Planning process or attend a workshop at the Life/Work Planning Center in Washington, D.C.  All of these are "non-pathological" in orientation.  They don't look for problems to solve, rather they emphasize and bring out awareness and appreciation of successes and achievements, strengths, skills, and competencies.

Identify what you want to do and perhaps be.  Quite often, as a result of an assessment process, clergy discover that they *are* in the right place and they don't need to make a change, at least not now.  Once you have determined *what* you want to do, then you will decide *how* to do what you want and *where*.[3]  The wonder of this process is that once you discover the valid options that are open to you, you are not only free to go somewhere new, you are also free to stay where you are!

Identify the negative people in your life and stay away from them. Include in your list of people to stay away from those who are usually considered friends of yours but who are essentially pessimistic about life, the church, and your situation.  Remember the flight of the Holy Family into Egypt to escape the agents of death.  There are some things, some people, from whom one ought to run away!

### 3. You are normal

What is happening to you is probably a perfectly normal and usual situation that clergy all over the nation face from time to time.  Men and women from all denominations are encountering similar job search tasks and problems, including the stress experienced.  The issue is not what is happening to you in this process, but how you relate to what is happening.  There is a time and place to address the complications and mysteries of what is happening to clergy in transition in the larger arena of our culture, but the least profitable time to address that larger subject is during your own job search.

Clergymen and women, in general, are persons of enormous competency, skill, and gifts. These skills and competencies are transferrable to an indefinite number of places both in and out of the church. It is this awareness, when it comes, that results in a sense of freedom. To know that about ourselves, or even to take it on faith, results in freedom. Remember: it is when you have gained the freedom to go that you also have the freedom to stay.

NOTES

1. From "God and Mankind: A Comparison of World Religions." Quoted by permission of The Teaching Company, Arlington, VA 22201.

2. For information, write: Registrar, Two Week Workshop, P.O. Box 379, Walnut Creek, CA 94597.

3. Richard Bolles, *What Color Is Your Parachute?* (Berkeley, CA: Ten Speed Press, 1990), 57.

## Section B: When a Clergyperson Is in Serious Trouble

What if you begin the job search in big trouble?

"Big trouble" in this context refers to imminent separation or dissolution of the employment contract or covenant or being accused of an action or behavior which is "actionable" in a civil, criminal, or ecclesiastical proceeding. "Big trouble" has to do with being accused, with being threatened, with being guilty, with not being guilty but being accused nonetheless, with being found out in some impropriety or being suspected of one. It may mean being charged with a felony, perhaps involving inappropriate handling of money or accusations of sexual improprieties by an adult or a minor.

"Big trouble" can include being accused by a counselee's spouse of alienation of affection when a separation or divorce is in progress. It may involve mistakes or perceived mistakes in pastoral, psychological, or spiritual counseling. Or it may involve an accusation of inadequate performance in one's duties or a change in behavior which others perceive to be too great for them to cope with. Any of these and many more, some too wild to imagine, may trigger a request for a resignation or may be the basis for an accusation or charges to be filed.

## Initial Assessment

If you think you are in "big trouble," there are certain steps to take and questions to ask. Assessing the problem is top priority. This is a fact-finding step. But first, ask yourself if you are in a good position to carry out this assignment. Is your anxiety level so high that perhaps your judgment is not adequate to the moment? If it is not, turn to one other person to be your companion in this lonely time.

### What is the nature of the crisis?

Is it inappropriate behavior in relationships, financial irregularities, or something more attuned to competency issues and adequacy in carrying out responsibilities? Has there been a secret meeting of the board of trustees or vestry including such statements as "He/she's not the right one for this congregation," "We think there was some misrepresentation back when the hiring took place," "Besides, a lot of us don't like his/her sermons." It can be quite difficult to identify just what some people think and feel and who it is that is generating discontent and/or making charges. It can take time and a lot of investigation.

Our perception of the nature of a crisis and the degree of difficulty involved can change in a matter of minutes, hours, or days by getting more information. Clerics who came to an early conclusion that a crisis of unmanageable proportions would end their ministry in their parish were able to continue successfully for many years, weathering the storm which initially appeared to have the power to wreck their pastoral relationship and leadership capacity. Some crises turn out to be just that, however, and it is important to understand as clearly as possible what the situation is and what it isn't.

From the patterns of firing in the past few years, it appears that perceived competency issues are the most common situations clergy in big trouble face. Significant numbers of clergy have been fired in recent years for no more serious cause than that some power clique didn't like their "style." Intimations, gossip or innuendo, and vague questions about what he or she does during the day may be employed by certain people to create a climate for separation.

## Damage Control

When accusations, firings, or suspensions occur they arrive in the form of a letter, a phone call, or occasionally in the form of a personal visit from someone in authority. Quite often the first notice a clergyperson will have about "big trouble" is in the indirect comment of someone who is not in authority but who heard it from someone who heard it from someone who heard it from someone else. In the midst of the sinking feelings, bewilderment, and possible rage that fill you, you will want to remember that damage control is the first order of business.

Important questions are these: "Is anything likely to happen in the next hour or two or day or two that would affect the life or limb of anyone, including yourself?" "Can this be prevented by some action you can take: making a phone call, for example, or having a meeting or doing something to ascertain the nature of this apparent catastrophe without making matters worse?"

Don't wait too long to take some kind of action. If everything is too confusing for you to make a confident decision, turn to someone you can trust for counsel, as described below.

## Taking Care of Yourself

How are you?  The answer may be "terrible."  Though you are accustomed to investing body, mind, and spirit in the care of others, taking care of yourself must now be an urgent priority.  Do you need medical or psychiatric help now or before the day is out?  Are you distraught?  Do you feel suicidal?  If so, do you know where to turn?  If you feel completely full of despair call 911 or call a doctor you know or your judicatory head.  Can you drive yourself to the hospital?  Who is the nearest person who can help you?  If any of these items add up to "Yes," go ahead and get the help.  If not, go on to the next item.

## Who Can I Talk To?  Who Should I Not Tell?

The answers to these questions depend partly on whether what you have done or are accused of doing is "actionable" in a criminal, civil, or ecclesiastical proceeding.  If so, proceed with caution.  You cannot be assured that your interests will be looked out for by persons who were heretofore close, intimate, and trusted colleagues.  Some of these persons have responsibilities which will require them to choose between supporting you or someone else and remaining neutral until the problem is solved (if it can be solved with you remaining in place).

You must use your judgment, of course, in all of these matters and with each of these persons.  Unfortunately, it is not uncommon for more dirty laundry to be aired for all to see than is necessary, increasing the scope of the problems to be solved.

*Consulting an attorney.*  If you are not sure about whether a problem is "actionable," you should consult a lawyer who is *not* associated with you or your organization.

---

### Testing Assumptions about Due Process

As a clergyperson you cannot assume that due process will be exercised if you have been accused.  You must take all the steps available to you to guarantee as much of your own well-being as you can.  You and your lawyer may be the only ones who will work for you when push comes to shove.

## Making an Initial Plan

Because of the way some people may respond to the news that there is a problem with possible moral, ethical, and or legal dimensions, consider carefully whom to tell about the problem and in what order. Those people you must tell whose responses have in the past been known to be reactionary, hysterical, or punitive should be told only after you have done as much as you can to assess the damage, and only after you have prepared your mind and heart as well as possible for an encounter with them.

Associates, colleagues, and staff. It is not always advisable to tell your staff associates or colleagues of the problem or of your part in the problem. Do not confess to them. They have a job to do in the same place where you are having this problem and they may not be in a good position to serve as your confidante and support. They will have to assume that role with lots of other people. If you need to make a confession, go to someone else.

Superiors. It is not always advisable to tell your judicatory head, your bishop, district superintendent or conference minister, or senior pastor right away. This person who has been your pastor in all other matters up to this moment may now be put into the position of being your judge. You may need to tell him or her, but think about how and when you will do so, considering how best to protect yourself.

In addition, your superior may not be particularly skilled in dealing with such important issues even though he or she has the responsibility to be involved ultimately. If there are precedents that indicate that he or she is, in fact, able to manage conflicted situations between clergy and congregations, then that information bears on your decision about when to discuss this with your superior.

Parish/congregational leaders. It is not always advisable to tell the parish leadership right away. It may be prudent to prepare your thoughts with the assistance of trusted advisors before going to the responsible leaders in your parish or organization. This is especially true if you anticipate a general communication to the whole constituency.

**Feelings You Will Need to Face**

It may take a lot of work and a little time to get in touch with your feelings: overwhelming shame, engulfment, the deepest sense of being at fault (even if you are wrongly or falsely accused), the feeling of "being bad," self-judgment, and self-punishment. You may find yourself thinking that you deserve all that is happening and the worst that might happen to you. To ask for help feels as though it will betray allegiance to the guilt and shame which seems richly deserved in this dark hour. The result feels like paralysis and helplessness.

Hurt and rage are common feelings in these situations. The hurt often stems from knowing that you have been betrayed by persons to whom you have given your life. The rage can erupt because of what people have said or done or not done. The sense of injustice in the situation may include being furious at not only those who may have done you wrong but also those who have not lifted a finger to stand by you or defend you. Strong feelings in all directions are understandable for a person who is in big trouble. Many of these feelings might tempt a person to turn inward, but don't do it!

## Drawing on Resources

DON'T "GO IT ALONE"
*Spiritual friends, professional friends, and others*

When you have completed the initial assessment and the damage control, there are additional steps to consider. As in all the other lonely places where clergy may find themselves, the sagest advice is to resist the temptation to deal with these matters alone. In the midst of great tension and conflict, our judgment is apt to be constricted and even impaired. In the heat and confusion and embarrassment of big trouble, one may be reluctant to ask others for help.

Here are some thoughts about possible resource persons and some services they may be able to offer you.

---

### Your Spiritual Resources

This can be a time to seek out spiritual guides and persons with a clear ethical sense in a way you never have before. When you are in such emotional, social, and spiritual straits it is often very hard to be grounded spiritually. This may be the place where your calling (vocation) gets truly integrated with the rest of your life. When time and energy and everything else allows, we will likely ask the question, "Am I still called to serve God with my skills, interests, and talents?"

### Where is God?

It may seem that the One who has been your companion and strength in your journey is absent or hard to locate in the midst of your trouble. If you have been neglecting this relationship it may not occur to you that God is a major source of strength and confidence. Turn to your spiritual center often and spend as much time there as is needed. Michael Dwinell, spiritual guide and psychotherapist, suggests that you "come apart before you come apart."

---

## Technical Advice from Professionals

Moral indignation and hurt feelings are no substitute for getting good expert advice and support for sorting out the essential from the extraneous. You can waste a lot of time by silently or publicly raging against your accusers. Whatever opinion you may have had of other professionals up to this time, you may need to turn to them for assistance now.

### Lawyers

Attorneys can often offer a lot more than straightforward advice about laws and statutes. They can also help sort out the emotional from the factual and help differentiate between substantive issues and related but unnecessary detail.

**Mediators/Arbitrators/Conflict Resolution Resources**

Mediation and arbitration is another route, but you should know that they
are not the same thing. Mediators attempt to bring conflicted parties
together so that each achieves as much of their respective goals as possible. Mediation and conflict resolution are very similar, relying on similar principles and resources. Persons trained in conflict resolution and
mediation can often bring all parties in a conflict or dispute to a win/win
posture and away from a win/lose posture. They may not help us fix the
problem or make it go away, but they can help each party get more of the
desired results which they are not likely to achieve unassisted.

*Levels of conflict.* Mediators and persons trained in conflict resolution
can, by interviewing the parties to a dispute, assess what level or degree
of conflict the dispute has reached. Some conflict theory suggests that
there are five levels ranging from disagreement (level one) to irreconci-
liable difference (level five). Not dealing with the problem or responding only negatively and reactively often exacerbates the situation. What
was a "level one" disagreement escalates into conflict of greater magni-
tude when ignored or fueled by emotion and polarization. Few conflicts
which are judged to be irreconcilable were always thus. Many opportunities for creative response are usually missed before reaching such a
state.

When appropriate resources are brought to bear, mostly in the person of outside mediators and consultants, many troubled relationships
can be improved. Clergy who initially felt they were in "big trouble"
find out that the situation can be addressed with constructive dialogue,
negoti-ation, and reconciliation.

Arbitrators are a third party resource to help two stymied parties
reach a resolution based on facts and rational arguments presented by
each side. An arbitrator will hear all the evidence and render a judgment.
Arbitration may or may not be binding. The types of arbitration would
be decided in the initial discussions of the parties with the arbitrator.

Whether the services of one of these skilled professionals is used
will be agreed upon by both parties, with as full an understanding as
possible of what is offered and what is possible and what isn't. To use
outside resources without full appreciation of the implications of their
involvement can lead to even greater and protracted conflict.

---

**About Hiring Professionals: Be prepared to pay.**
Inquire as to what the costs will be for an attorney's services.
This information will help you assess any financial impact a situation might have for you. Occasionally professionals offer reduced fees or pro bono services. Whatever the financial arrangement, you will want to be in a position to make appropriate demands on your attorney and not feel bashful because he or she is doing you a favor. This can be an instance which illustrates the adage "you get what you pay for." When you need it, get good legal assistance, someone who will work assertively for you.

---

## Other Resources

### a. Persons with moral and persuasive authority in the community

This is the role of the elder or sage whose history qualifies him or her to bring healing and resolution to a conflict. This is a nonlitigious relationship bound by history and affiliation. It has at its base the good will and long-term well-being of the whole community. Taking initiative to communicate with such persons and to urge them to overcome personal reluctance to get involved can represent initiative on your part to move the situation along to speedier resolution and in a spirit of constructive compromise.

This resource needs to be used with caution by clergy since these persons often have a history of loyalty to the community. They may themselves get emotionally hooked into the outcome and prejudice the outcome to the benefit of their oldest affiliations. On the other hand, their magnanimity can transcend allegiance, and they are in a position to propose trade-offs and solutions that parties to conflict cannot see.

### b. Good problem solvers

Folks who are not professional mediators or arbitrators but who have demonstrated a cool levelheadedness in other kinds of problem solving can be brought in to facilitate matters that do not involve civil or criminal law. Usually optimistic but matter-of-fact in their approach, they can add a dispassionate presence which others may trust.

c. <u>Friends of the parties and advocates for the community</u>
People who care about one or both parties and the community to which
they both belong can in some cases be helpful in sorting out disputes and
conflicts which have not advanced too far. This may be a "friendly inter-
vention" made with good will and common sense. Some disputes begin
to feel more serious than they need to because time passes with no
change in the attitudes of the parties. A kind of entrenchment sets in. A
good-spirited gesture by such a friend, sometimes adding a prayerful
spirit or a sense of humor, can break a logjam that was destined to move
to more serious dimensions.

They use up their "credit" in such interventions and the effectiveness of their efforts will be known rather quickly. Usually they can inter-
vene with disputants only once or twice. This may be a temporary or
"space-creating" gesture on their part, providing breathing space for
more substantial problem-solving activities to begin.

## Summary

One of the hardest things to do when in "big trouble" is to get to the
place where we can talk with others and draw on their strength, faith,
skill, and expertise in spite of our self-consciousness, possible embarrassment, and confusion. You can do it however. Whether you turn to
persons like those named above or some others you think of, please remember: just don't deal with your big trouble alone.

# Attitudes and Strategies for Survival and Beyond

Clergy who are in any kind of trouble will probably find it difficult to be
anything but defensive in the technical sense of the term. Many people
do not find it in their nature to go on the offensive with counter charges
and counter suits. Here are some thoughts about whether to choose a
defensive or offensive posture when in big trouble.

## On the Defense

When charges are leveled, the accused instinctively and reasonably
moves toward a posture of defending herself or himself. If a lawyer you
have engaged seems to have an implicit faith in the "good will of church
people" or a belief that "this isn't too serious" and "reasonable people
will surely be able to work this out," you may want to consider getting a

second opinion or hiring a different lawyer. You want someone in your employ for your defense who is unequivocally on your side and who will want to see evidence of "good will" before trusting in it.

### On the Offense

It is terribly hard for clergy to consider going on the offense when accused. Having spent your professional life preaching about the kingdom of heaven and trying to believe in the beatitudes, it just doesn't seem right that you should ever get in a position where you would be accusing someone in your congregation. Going on the offense often means accusing someone else in the form of a counter suit. When serious charges are levelled against you, you will of course want to try to find every other reasonable avenue for resolution. At the same time, playing hard ball without a mitt on your hand is likely to result in significant injury. Serious charges should be met with a serious response. Try your best to avoid the appearance of accepting any punishment your accusers may wish to mete out to you. The inner resolve for serious defense often means going on the offense.

Clergy, believing that the problem will go away, often wait too long before taking seriously the fact that they and their lawyer or other representatives need to make their reasonable, morally and legally available options known to their accusers. Issues of libel, defamation of character, mutual responsibility for circumstances and conditions giving rise to conflict, and the potentially high cost of settlement all need to be considered. Lawyers can help think these things through. Don't wait too long.

## Conclusion

### A Future in the Church?

"Do I have a future in the church?" you may ask yourself. The most amazing part of all of this is that you do have a future. You will live again. In all but a few instances, clergy who have fallen on hard times such as these do in fact recover, make a new start, and make a positive contribution to the church or other setting where they choose to exercise their skills and competencies.

This new start may not come until after you have experienced the worst that the church has to hand out, however. Who would want anything to do with people or institutions who treat you badly? Sadly, religious institutions are sometimes pathological in their treatment of clergy. Churches often use up pastors and, when they are in trouble, abandon them like wounded soldiers to die beside the road. It has been said that the church sometimes shoots its wounded instead of dealing with them compassionately, with understanding, forgiveness, and reconciliation.

## You Have a Future

In spite of these harsh facts, this same institution that exists to extol the mercy, grace, and forgiveness of God often does exhibit a curious combination of forgiveness and loss of memory toward those who have had big trouble while in ministry. Given some time and perhaps a change of place, continuation of or restoration to ministry and beginning again does take place. The question of your future doesn't have to be answered in detail right now—just know that there is a future and a full life, however many wounds there are for you now. The resurrection applies to you too.

## Section C: The Clergyperson with Disability

## What Do We Know?

Across the nation and in all denominations men and women are experiencing life-changing accidents and illnesses that render them "disabled." As medical technology progresses and health services improve, and as the effects of accident and illness are minimized, there is strong evidence that the numbers of persons who will be "disabled" in some way during their working years (before the time they normally would retire) is increasing significantly.

The next few years will be a time of restructuring the churches' attitudes, programs, and policies regarding clergy who have disabilities. The effect of 1990 federal legislation, tightening regulations around discrimination against those with disabilities, will have an impact on society. It is not yet clear that the legislation will affect clergy in any direct way, but it is bound to create greater awareness and sensitivity. The implications of this legislation are significant and give great hope to the millions of persons who are in some way "disabled." What about the clergywoman or man? Clergy face the same difficulties of emotional, spiritual, and social adjustment as persons in other professions, and maybe some special ones as well. Church leaders and congregations face a major challenge to find new ways to honor and utilize the gifts and talents of clergy who have disabilities.

**What do we mean by disability?**

In general, and for the purposes of this chapter, we can assume that the disabled include: persons who are in relatively sustainable, stable conditions but whose workplace skills, abilities, or capabilities have been altered in some way and persons whose work skills, abilities, or capabilities will be affected over time by a condition of gradual or eventual deterioration and diminishment of function.

**How does one become disabled?**

One can become disabled in a variety of ways. Disability can be the result of a physical condition, such as a heart attack, stroke, asthma, emphysema, neurological disorder, or Alzheimers. A disability could be the loss of mobility from an accident or a hearing loss or blindness resulting from natural causes or accident.

Disability can also result from emotional, neurological, and/or physical limitations caused by a blow on the head or a fall. It can also be a diminishment of capacity to function as a result of trauma or work-related stress.

Disability can result from experiencing a major loss. The death or loss of a lifelong companion, for example, can seriously disrupt one's life to the point of minimal functioning.

Disability can result from alcoholism, drug, or substance abuse or degenerative disease.

The questions which emerge from these types of disabilities are: first, how does the clergyperson respond to and manage the new realities that result from having or developing a disability? And second, how does the clergyperson who has a "disability" continue in a career-related activity?

## How Does the Clergyperson Respond to the New Reality?

Who me? Surely there is some mistake! There must be something that can be done to restore me to the level of functioning I previously enjoyed! One disbelieving and disorienting sensation after another generates questions that have a ring of unreality about them. But here I am. Life has really changed for me!

The adjustments to a disability are significant. Obvious effects, such as body changes, wheelchairs, walking assistance, reliance on others for communication or other basic needs, represent major changes with which one has to deal. There will be an apparently endless succession of adjustments, from the length of time it takes to do things to navigating the shallow waters of public acceptance.

A person discovers early on, as he or she begins to come to terms with disability, that the stages of grief apply. Shock, disbelief, rage and anger, attempts to fix it, bargaining, depression and possibly acceptance are all part of the range of feelings that are experienced.

Attempting to focus on the implications of a newly discovered limitation can result in something like a fog or general confusion; the most daunting aspect may be experiencing isolation, role ambiguity, or what may best be described as psychic, spiritual pain. One's first response is to want to fix it or to get rid of it, as many of us have done with any sickness or physical impairment, such as the flu or a broken rib.  We certainly don't want to hear that we can't "get rid of it."

A person might spend some time finding new variations on what it means to be in denial of reality.  These could include forms of distorted thinking, avoidance, planning as though nothing had happened, or chasing after cures.  Little by little the realization dawns that "the real issue is not what has happened but how I relate to what is happening."

The effect of a disabling accident or illness on the family, co-workers, and the congregation is upsetting and bewildering.  As the person with the disability goes through trauma and discomfort, all the people around him or her will go through pain and anxiety as well, but it will be in their own way and out of the context of their own lives, needs, and concerns.  Some will be able to set aside their own immediate needs and interests and minister to the person with the disability, but others will not.

The feeling of a loss of choice has a significant impact on one's adjustment to a disability.  There may be a desperate sense that choices are running out and that freedom previously known and cherished is forever lost.  Life is now interdependent with others in a new way.  This reality may affect one's sense of independence and result in a general feeling that career options are nearly nonexistent.

Even in the early stages of disability, there are multiple and complex factors at work.  In unformed and unshaped ways, issues of identity, public image, and self-esteem are involved.  Depending on the nature of the disability and whether or not there is a change in physical appearance, mobility, or other factors that affect our public image, one's self-esteem may be undermined.

Experiencing a life-changing accident or illness surely affects one's whole life.  Personal identity, relationships, day-to-day living, and career are affected.  What follows is offered to help minimize the damage and to emphasize the life-giving possibilities.

## How Does the Clergyperson Manage the New Reality?

### Attitudes

Coping with a major life change caused by illness or accident includes addressing not only physical or emotional aspects but also attitudes.  Exploring and being aware of these attitudes may not eliminate them, but it can demystify them and enable us to transcend them.

An examination of attitudes is important for the person experiencing disability, for ignoring them can seriously limit recovery from an illness or an accident. Very often the desire to recover is diminished or squelched when one encounters assumptions that a person who has a disability is helpless, is to be pitied, or is less able to take his or her place in "normal" society. One cannot afford to be demoralized by negative attitudes; there is too much at stake. A positive attitude is essential for developing skills for daily living, maintaining social activity, and pursuing purposeful work.

## The Problem with Language

For the longest time there was no apparent problem with referring to people with certain limitations as disabled or handicapped people. Most well-meaning people who used such terminology only meant to describe what those with a disability experienced or to acknowledge what were perceived to be real and important changes or conditions in their lives. In time sensitivity to de facto discrimination stemming from illogical and prejudicial assumptions manifested in the use of words has caused us to see what cruel and unnecessary barriers are erected for great numbers of people with disability.

There have been important developments in semantics in recent years. "Handicapped" and "mentally retarded" are being replaced by a more humanistic and less dehumanizing terminology reflecting an understanding that persons affected by accident or illness are persons first and that they have a disability second. Thus, the term "handicap" has been changed to "disability" in the literature and discussion of the present.[1]

The difference in such language may appear superficial and subtle at first, but it reflects a radical reorientation of public attitude towards millions of people. These changes in attitude in public schools and in society at large are beginning to find expression in churches. Stewart Govig, in *Strong at the Broken Places, Persons with Disabilities and the Church*, suggests "instead of the words disabled, handicapped, crippled, paralyzed, retarded, and impaired, perhaps I should use the words disAbled, (dis)abled, dis/abled, dis(en)abled, physically challenged, or differently abled."[2]

Focusing on the person rather than the limitation is a major accomplishment in the life of anyone who has experienced a life-changing illness or accident. Developing a new vocabulary and learning to apply it can make a big difference. Instead of considering oneself "disabled" a person might think and speak of differently-abled or temporarily-able persons. The use of such language can be the precursor of new attitudes. Such modifications in our language and thinking will help us to realize that all of us have limitations.

Such progress is important and promises a new future for persons with disabilities in our society, but still there is much to be done.

## Attitudes about Clergy and Disability

Some clergy have been shocked to discover how little members of their congregation and even their clergy colleagues have been able to relate and empathize with them. If the onset of the disability is sudden, parishioners, friends, and family are understandably uninformed and even bewildered about what is going on and what the future holds. The emotional effect can be devastating to them. But encountering the emotional reactions of others may only deepen the isolation and loneliness of the person who has the disability. Education and information will be needed to help others arrive at a new place where they can be present, unanxious, and companionable.

Attitudes in church institutions towards those with disabilities have been changing. In the early days of pension funds and disability benefits, many (perhaps most) claims for disability benefits submitted by clergy were granted. In many denominations, only one signature of an Area Pastor, Superintendent, or Bishop was needed, with little or no corroborating documentation or expert opinion required. Now as many as four signatures may be required, reflecting the same number of committees which have reviewed documentation and claims. Confidential psychological and medical records may need to be included in the review as well.

In the past decade clergy have attempted to solve a number of personal and career related problems by applying for disability. These included tired and worn out clergy who, when approaching retirement age, learned that heart conditions, arthritis, or emotional fatigue were sufficient basis to claim disability. In some cases there was a "bonus" for retiring with disability. A number of clergy who had become ineffective because of dysfunction of one kind or another, including social ineptitude, have been "put out to pasture" by judicatory officials who didn't know what else to do with them. Such marginal or inappropriate uses of disability funds clearly added to the set of conditions for justification of claims which a genuinely disabled person faces today. At best, a clergyman or woman will find sympathy and smooth sailing through a claims process; at worst, he or she will find suspicion and hostility from claims review investigators and board members.

## Assessment and Prayer

In addition to addressing and managing the attitudes reflected in use of language, administration of pension funds, and reactions of friends and parishioners, there are two other endeavors to take to heart in managing the new reality of a disability: getting a thorough assessment and re-membering to pray.

### *Assessment*

Assessment by professionally trained persons is needed. Good, basic information is available from professional diagnosticians and caretakers who have plenty of experience in the light of which they can compare your present situation with the best that can be hoped for. Each disci-pline has something to offer which may not be known to other practi-tioners, and it is worth the time and trouble to go to as many different types of caregivers as is possible. Self-assessment or assessment by family members or peers is not adequate.

### *Second Opinions*

As a part of the assessment process a second opinion may be appropriate and should be sought in a timely fashion without embarrassment or apology to one's initial caregiver. In any matter affecting one's health or daily functioning, it is professionally acceptable to expect that the initial or primary caregivers, including physicians and therapists, will provide names and contacts for second opinions. In most cases insurance com-panies will pay for and even require a second opinion.

### *Prayer*

Clergy are sometimes the last persons who remember to pray about their own needs in adversity. It needs to be said that spiritual reflection and prayer are among the primary resources in such times. Meeting the chal-lenge of pain, trauma, and major life change, for a short or much longer time, will probably confront and test one's faith perspective and relation-ship to God. This is not a time to "go it alone." Ask others to pray for and with you. Talk with someone about the spiritual dimensions of this new reality and its effect on you.

Making a new study of biblical images, stories, and personal understanding of who God is and what Jesus is all about will be useful. A major resource for this is to be found in Stewart Govig's *Strong at the Broken Places.*[3]

Managing the new reality of a disability by making good use of assessment and prayer lays the groundwork for moving on to the career issues that people with disability face. Unless we come to terms with attitudes reflected in language, responses of family members, colleagues and parishioners, realities of the bureaucratic red tape, we are likely to be stymied in our efforts to adjust to career challenges and obstacles. Consciously dealing with this set of issues makes moving on somewhat easier.

## Moving On: Identifying the Challenges and Obstacles

People with disabilities have discovered that their career issues are secondary to the concerns of a basic reorientation toward living on a daily basis, reestablishing relationships, and developing a sustainable lifestyle. True as this may be, ignoring or failing to take seriously future career issues shortchanges the possibilities. Before exploring the possibilities, however, it is useful to be aware of some of the obstacles and challenges that may arise. Recognizing their existence can reduce the power they otherwise have to trip you up. What follows is only a partial list of fundamental barriers. They have to do with personal identity, role identity, institutional connections and relationships, and other struggles.

### Questions and Issues about Personal Identity

Who am I? I begin to see how much of my identity and self-image have been tied to what I have done in my role as pastor and religious leader. Some part of me wants to believe that my worth is not tied to what I do, but who I am (in whatever shape or condition I find myself now). Another part of me discovers and realizes that I may have been investing my work and public roles with an inordinate amount of meaning and value.

You may need to talk with someone about sorting out these identity questions. Differentiating self from role is a critical exercise, not only for those with disabilities but for everyone.

**Questions and Issues About Belonging and Role Identity**

Issues of organizational commitment and the ability to conceptualize a
future in the kind of ministry roles available to you are likely to be at
stake. Will I continue my work as a pastor? Can I see myself in a modified role at all? Can I face the effect of the limitation my disability represents? Will my superiors endorse me in new, amended, or modified
expressions of my calling and vocation or will they want me to be like
everyone else? Will there be flexibility among the lay leadership and
those who have the moral and persuasive authority in the congregation to
reconceptualize my ministry with them?

    These concerns are among the most foundational. They have to do
with one of our strongest needs, which is belonging. They also have to
do with loyalty and commitment. Sorting these out will be basic to all
other career considerations.

**Questions and Issues and Worries Relating to Our Institutional
Connections**

Often, as such questions occur, memories of the most reactive and un-
kind responses we have witnessed in the church come to mind. Will the
least generous of our sisters and brothers in both the denomination and
the congregation end up having some determinative say in what happens
to me later? As we begin to consider what this disability means personally and professionally, fears based on past experience may move us
quickly into an emotional quagmire characterized by doubt and fore-
boding.

    These are valid concerns and questions. This is no place to stop,
however. There are practical steps to take to assess career objectives
which will be consistent with one's capabilities. There are lots of
options.

# Moving On to New Ways of Thinking

The barriers which people with disability (and others) experience are
often emotional and mental ones. One of life's consistent ironies is that
the greatest limitations on our capacities exist mostly in our own thinking
about what we can do.

## Some Struggles You May Encounter Along the Way

Legal struggles: Insurance companies, pension funds, and disability review committees represent decision making by people we never met, who don't know us, and who can determine much of our future. We may need to gather and present evidence to influence our own case in our favor in these decision processes.

You have already faced or will soon encounter the attitudes of those persons in positions of responsibility with authority to make decisions that affect your employment and that can be made in a way that affects you adversely.

You will encounter the dilemma of choosing and choice making vs. deference to authority and systems. It is vital that you not leave your future up to someone else who in all likelihood will be, at best, conservative and nonrisk-oriented—a posture that could result in unemployment or underemployment.

Someone, perhaps a colleague, your boss (if you are on the staff of a parish or an agency), or a judicatory staff person, may suggest or imply that there is little likelihood of your returning to work any time soon. It may come across in a comment like this: "Well, I can't think of any place for you now; maybe we will be able to figure something out as we go along." Many people have never thought about disabilities, so it is natural for him or her to say, "I can't think of any place for you right now." You may have to either ignore such comments and opinions and/or struggle in a constructive, thought-provoking way to stimulate thinking in others that will surface new possibilities.

Sooner or later you will apply for disability benefits if you have such coverage at all. Surprisingly and tragically, many church staff insurance packages do not include any such coverage. Assuming you do have disability coverage, *a disability review board* ill attempt to assess: 1) degree of disability, whether partial or total; 2) length of disability, whether short-term or continuing; 3) the nature of the problem, whether medical, psychological, or a dysfunction for other reasons; and 4) whether the disability prevents a person from all work or just some work. In addition, there will be a look at the possibility of preexisting conditions and whether there is reason to deny a claim or to grant it in spite of preexisting conditions. At the outset, many of these considerations will seem trite and insensitive to a disabled person and to his or her family and friends. To learn a new technical language related to pension fund detail and technicalities and to respond to the custodians of such funds, whose concerns stem from their years of experience with hundreds of other claims for disability benefits, will in itself add stress. All of this is likely to require great patience even as you make an assertive case for your claims for benefits and services.

The nine-dot game, which has been so often used in human development workshops or management courses, illustrates this point. The challenge in this game is to connect all nine dots using no more than four straight lines, without lifting your pencil or retracing any line. Try it.

•    •    •

•    •    •

•    •    •

Hard to do? If you know the exercise from previous experience or if you quickly see how to solve the puzzle, then you know that it is only by drawing lines extending outside the boundaries of the square of dots that the task can be accomplished. If we try to complete this task by moving no further than the outer edges of the design we will not be able to meet the challenge. On the other hand, by extending some of the lines well beyond the simple boundaries of the design, we can draw a line connecting all the dots without lifting the pencil or retracing any line.

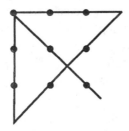

This exercise is, of course, a metaphor for what it takes to meet many of life's challenges. Learning to live with disabling effects of accident or illness can require that we think in new ways, ways which extend beyond the normal and usual boundaries of our problem-solving habits. What is important to remember from this little exercise is that what seems impossible, completely baffling, and frustrating can be accomplished with a new perspective and new approaches.

## Exploring Your Options:
## Role Models, Programs, and Style Options

A top priority is to begin to discover our real options for purposeful work, none of which means retiring, retreating, or disappearing.

You may wish to launch into your discovery of possibilities at the earliest possible moment. There are at least three directions in which to go exploring that could provide you with both inspiration and practical information: first, finding people who have been there before you; second, tracking down programs offering guidance and direction; and third, exploring new styles for your ministry.

### 1. People: A Source of Ideas and Inspiration

There are a lot of people who have been somewhere close to where you are. They have gone before you in some way in the world of disability and discovered or created purposeful work. You will notice accounts of such people more now than you ever did before and your research will uncover many. There is space here to mention only a few.

For example, there was the rector of one of the largest Episcopal parishes in Washington, D.C. who, after throat surgery in the middle of his career, spent the rest of his life "speaking" in a way which sounded different than before. Though his voice changed significantly and was severely impaired, he learned how to "speak" in a new way and preached regularly and powerfully each Sunday. In fact, parishioners say that they listened more intently to what he said. He continued his active ministry until he chose retirement in later years.

There is also the man who did group work, sensitively listening to every word of thousands of men and women year after year, who lost his hearing so that he could no longer do the work which was his life and joy. After he had recovered to a functional level, he built a support group of people interested in his field and began writing, putting on paper his precious insights and wisdom for others to read.

There is the account of the recovering alcoholic who, after a lengthy hospitalization and extensive therapy, took his first position in a smaller parish and then after a succession of positions, assumed responsibilities and a level of productivity approximately equal to his previous work.

A woman who became a paraplegic uses a special wheelchair to go around the country conducting workshops and motivational meetings for the tens of thousands, who like her, live with a disability. Her life is characterized by joy and spiritual freedom as she radiates purposefulness and energy for living.

There are numerous examples of persons who, in discovering that there was little understanding, sensitivity, or support for persons with disabilities, have developed chaplaincies and speaking ministries to the large numbers of persons like them who need advice, support, encouragement, and a sympathetic presentation of Scripture applied to their special interests and needs.

### 2. Programs:  A Way to Think about the Pursuit of Your Career Options
What are the employment potentials of those with disabilities?  What others have done may inspire you, but the real answer to this question begins in the assessment of who *you* are.  What is it *you* want to do?  It is important to begin this career transition at the same place that you would have begun a transition in your career if nothing had ever happened. That doesn't mean denying the reality of what's happened or acting as if nothing has changed.  Rather, it means starting with the same kind of attitude, energy, and hope you had in previous times.

Perhaps the most helpful way to get in touch with what you want to do is to look at what Bernard Haldane called "motivated skills."  Motivated skills are those transferrable skills we use wherever we are, whether on the job, in leisure, at home or away, or on our day off.  We enjoy using these skills over and over again.  These skills can be found in list form in Dick Bolles' *What Color Is Your Parachute?* and also in *The New Quick Job Hunting Map* which is a series of exercises excerpted from *Parachute*.[4]

It is useful to observe that clergy probably have the largest number of transferrable skills of all the professions.  As a result, clergy in general can move from parish ministry to an endless number of fields of employment including human services, managerial and organizational positions in governmental agencies, nonprofit enterprises (which, by the way, doesn't mean they have no money to pay salaries for executive level staff), and many industries and corporations.

As you look at the lists in some of the Bolles' resource books, you will see that they are divided into People oriented skills, Information oriented skills and Things oriented skills.  Most People and Information oriented skills can find expression in myriad places and opportunities.  A simple exploration of your skills is likely to reveal that your interests remain much the same as they were, your motivated skills (the ones you love to use) are mostly the same, and what remains to be discovered is whether or not you can continue to use them in the same place where you have been working until now. If not, then, it is time to dare a new thing: to create a new context in which to do what you love to do.

Our mission in life is to pursue those areas of activity and interest that are, first, tied to something that needs doing; second, tied to what we want to do (and enjoy doing); and third, perceived as contributing to what God seeks to accomplish in the world, even a little part of it.

A simple theological notion found in a brief exegesis of the word "enthusiasm" helps us to appreciate this idea. The root of *enthusiasm* is two Greek words *en* and *theos*—in God. I suggest that when we know ourselves to be enthusiastic about something we have done, are doing now, or might do in the future, this is the place where the creative intentional energy of God meets us in our own uniqueness. The task for all of us, with or without disability, is to discover the patterns of our enthusiasms, identify what it would mean to continue in this activity and to raise up such a vision to the level of our intention and goal for future activity. Once that is done, or when we have begun to make good progress on such wonderful discoveries; then we have laid the cornerstone of our career path and activity for the future.

### 3. Recovering and Increasing Choices: Consider Changing Your Style of Ministry

New possibilities for doing ministry as a person with disability may lie in a change in our ministry style. Many clergy, especially in parish ministry, have been "lone rangers," doing all of the preaching, pastoring, and administration by themselves. Not especially adept at developing team ministries, clergy have often harbored certain responsibilities and kept key tasks of ministry in their own personal portfolios.

Disability may make the lone ranger style of job performance impossible, if not forever, at least for the time being. To the degree that this may have been your style, it may be very difficult to make a transition to a team ministry. And yet, it may be that your future ministry depends upon a work setting in which you do just part of a whole set of tasks rather than continuing in your accustomed style of going it alone. A more collaborative, interdisciplinary style of ministry with both clergy colleagues and laity may not only result in a desirable new level of cooperation but may afford the only possibility for ministry. Developing a new appreciation of self-management skills and accepting a new interactive style of leadership can be a healthy sign.

4. <u>Transitional Positions: Occupational Therapy and Retraining</u>
One of the chief frustrations felt when one is knocked out of the job ring is having to get right back in it, yet concluding that's not possible.  In this case, it can help enormously to look at the next job or work role as transitional.  This can be a time to experiment, to develop a new understanding of yourself, and to learn how to manage relationships with people who think in the same old ways.  The first and perhaps the next position may be viewed as an opportunity to position yourself for moving toward the kind of position you want for the long term.

If you are not sure what kind of work you want to do or are capable of doing, occupational therapy can introduce you to areas of work that you never considered before and that will provide opportunities to use and develop skills and competencies.  It can also help you strategize how to join a team or how to start out part-time or begin work on a limited schedule.  Occupational therapy can help you develop new self-management skills and even build a support group to assist on practical levels.

*Retraining* (and developing latent interests) might be one of the avenues to developing a career path when one cannot do all the many interdisciplinary tasks that used to get done.  If you enjoyed counseling individuals, couples, or families, for example, advanced academic work and supervision by a licensed and experienced counselor or therapist may allow you to focus on that ministry.  If you are good at administration and management, some further training may allow you to emphasize these skills in parishes, agencies, or organizations of which you would enjoy being a part and which would value your competence and gifts.  If your mobility has been affected in a significant way, it may be helpful to remember that *many people can come to you.*

## Conclusion

Laying the groundwork for the future is work!  Use the hours and days and weeks engaged in pursuing the future as a time to go to work in all the ways you can, developing perspective, managing resources, saying your prayers, and paying attention to the other ways that feed your spiritual center.  Try to allocate definite amounts of time on a daily and weekly basis for focusing these matters.  Set goals for developing a schedule for working on career adjustments, new experiments, and transitions.  Keep a record of all that you do including ideas you have, phone calls you make, persons to talk to, and accounts of conversations and meetings held. All of this can be significantly useful for future reference.

Experiencing adversity from illness or accident resulting in disability can be among the most difficult experiences of life. Dealing with our career in this context may present challenges we never thought possible. In the midst of the loneliness, the pain, and the plethora of radical adjustments that our goals require of us, we will be called forward into a new place, even as we remain essentially the person we always were. For people of deep and active faith this can be the time and place in which we integrate our sense of vocation, call, and belief into a deeper maturity where the words of scripture, the teachings of our faith, and life in community take on new meaning.

NOTES

1. Brolin and Gysbers, "Career Education for Students with Disabilities," *Journal of Counseling & Development*, Volume 68, No. 2, Nov.-Dec., 1989, p. 155.

2. Stewart Govig, *Strong at the Broken Places, Persons with Disabilities and the Church*, (Louisville, KY: Westminster/John Knox Press, 1989, p. 2.

3. Ibid. Each of eight chapters has many scriptural references to those who have experienced accident or illness.

4. Richard Bolles, op. cit. (Part 1), pp. 76, 78.

Also Richard Bolles, *The New Quick Job-Hunting Map*, op. cit., 1979, 1985, pp. 13-21.

SOURCES AND REFERENCES

*Strong at the Broken Places, Persons with Disabilities and the Church* by Steward D. Bovig, Westminster/John Knox Press, Louisville, KY, 1989.

"People with Disabilities:  An Update," by Eagan and Jenkins, *Journal of Counseling & Development*, Volume 68, No. 2, Nov.-Dec. 1989.

"Role of Counseling in Enabling Persons with Disabilities," by Charles W. Humes, Edna Mora Szymanski, and Thomas H. Hohenshil, *Journal of Counseling & Development*, Volume 68, No. 2, Nov.-Dec., 1989.

CHAPTER IV

# Getting Support:
# What Kind, Why, and How

*by Loren B. Mead*

Quite a lot is said about getting "support," having a "support group," during the period of job search. I would like to say something about this: what *kind* of support, why, and how to get it. I am not talking about hand-holding. At least not yet.

## Technical Support

There are a lot of things most of us are not up to date on. Fashions change radically in how resumes are drawn up, and each denomination has its own forms and methods for circulating names. Anybody serious about seeking a position needs to be conversant with the best and most up-to-date techniques and skills. Check your judicatory office or national deployment office. Often you can get good free consultation. You also need to *know* the fads and terminology people are using around the country and whether or not you use them. Career centers sometimes provide consultation on this.

## Personal Assessment

You need a clearer picture of your areas of strength and weakness than most of us have from day to day. Books (Bolles' *What Color Is your Parachute?* or Miller's chapter in this book) have designs you can use to get that clarity. You may prefer to be in a structured group where you can be led through the designs and helped toward clarity in dialogue with others. I find the latter works best for me. Again, that is a strength of the career centers. Career advisors can do this, too, but be sure they know *church* systems. I have known groups of clergy to contract with each other for such work, using Bolles or some other guide. Some kinds of parish or clergy assessment can help you get clear about your strengths and weaknesses.

## The Process Itself

There are places in the search process at which special help can make a difference. Check out *any* written communication to the prospective "job" with a friend or consultant, not for their approval but for hard critique. Don't take offense at criticism, no matter how harsh. Use a friend or consultant to prepare for interviews. With their help get clear about what you want to communicate and how you can demonstrate your own strengths in an interview format. You may even want to design the interview (many search committees get anxious and arrive for an interview with little clarity about how to proceed—you may be able to help them). Ask for help in debriefing every contact with the prospective job or committee. Your friend/consultant can help you pick up clues that you may want to follow up. At worst, you will learn how to do interviews better in the future.

## Your Own Personal Needs

When things are toughest for *me*, there are two things I just have to do or I'll go crazy: (1) I make sure I get to the mid-week worship I go to almost every week, where somebody else is "in charge" (for me, it's a holy communion service) and (2) I make liberal use of the book of Psalms (my reason, if I need one, is that that's the book Jesus seems to have used when things got tough for him). What I want to communicate through this gratuitous self-disclosure is that I have to find my own personal way to my spiritual roots—the way that fits *me*.

I'm telling you to pay attention during this time to the places in your religious tradition where you get fed. That may be the most important support. As always, it's easy to let this drop. Don't. It's the heart of your search and the best support you can get.

Your personal anxiety about a job can energize you to do what you need to do, but it can also be your worst enemy if you let it get out of hand. Stay close to the people you know are behind you. Count on your spouse (but also be realistic about how he or she, too, may need help through this time). Don't hesitate to use a counsellor, pastor, or therapist.

Your anxiety, if it's not under control, can lead you to take a job that really doesn't fit you or to sell yourself so hard the people don't see the real "you."

**Two Special Times of Need**

1. <u>Rejection</u>. Most people get turned down more than they get selected. Don't kid yourself. Also, don't expect rejection to feel good. Don't be surprised if it really knocks you for a loop. However it is phrased, whatever the reality actually is, it *feels* like rejection and it feels awful. All our old tapes run overtime—the time you were chosen last for the team, the time you did not get asked to the dance, the day your name was omitted from the list. Give yourself space to grieve. Watch out for what you say and do to the "rejecting congregation" or to your bishop or exec. Blow up if you have to. Cry if you have to. Cuss them out if you have to. But do it with close friends—*not* to the people who rejected you, *not* in public situations.

2. <u>Weariness and Loss of Hope</u>. This comes after several rejections. Its real name is depression, and it can be a bear. Staying *with* people, keeping plans up and moving, using each rejection as an opportunity to learn—all are important. Do what you have to to stay in the game. Friends are essential. One activity that can be very helpful is consciously seeking help in reassessing your current work. *Sometimes* a "no" to a call elsewhere may be a clue that you are called to stay where you are.

**Your Current Work**

The most important thing in seeking new work is to keep giving your current work real commitment. The framework of support there—the congregation and its leaders, your family and friends, your religious life —should be the basic support system to which you add those things specially needed as you search for a new job. Be sensitive about how your parishioners feel if they hear you are "looking." At the right time take key leaders into your confidence, but it probably is not best to broadcast every nibble!

*A Final Word*

You are not looking for a job. You are looking for the right place to invest your personal gifts and graces in God's service.

The systems within which we work are flawed and imperfect, to say the least.  You will experience a lot of those imperfections as you go through the search.

Remember that you are searching for a call, a vocation.  And there are people out there somewhere who want to share their vocation with you.  Maybe it won't be what you expected.

So hang on.

# CHAPTER V

# What's the Matter with That Church— Are They Stalling or What?

*What's going on while you wait impatiently by the phone.*

*by Loren B. Mead*

## Introduction to the Issue

One of the characteristic problems that seems to hit clergy when they get into the job search these days is the terrible long silences that come.

A phone call from a congregation comes out of the blue, asking if you would permit your name to be considered (some may even put it as "be a candidate"). Many clergy in one way or another say "Yes."

Nothing happens.

A reference calls you and says the congregation you've been in correspondence with has called them and seemed very interested.

Nothing happens.

A judicatory office tells you, "They are putting together a profile, but they aren't ready to receive names yet. Give them another month."

Nothing happens.

You hear that you "made the final cut."

Nothing happens.

All through the process, the clergyperson feels as if some kind of stall is on. Long silences. Hidden activities.

One of the results has been a buildup of resentment among many clergy I know. Around clergy meetings one hears angry words about "The Process." It's thought to be too long, poorly handled, or just awful in general. The anger leaks over onto the denomination's procedures or offices for helping clergy placement. If there is any computer involved, it often becomes the chief culprit.

I discovered some time ago that there is a very simple answer to why this happens.

No clergyperson ever really experiences what a congregation experiences in what we used to call a "vacancy."

What I want to do in this chapter is to help clergy get a handle on what is going on in the congregation that makes those long silences make a lot of sense.

I think clergy who understand what is happening in the congregation will be more able to respond positively to the needs of the congregation, knowing better when it is appropriate to push and when to wait. It may also make the waiting a bit more bearable.

One added theological note. This is an important distinction. Ministry in that congregation belongs to the people, not to the pastor—within, of course, the traditions of that denomination. But the impatience of the clergy often masks a kind of imperial concept of ministry—that there really isn't any ministry in the congregation until they have a clergy-person there. Most who are impatient with the wait do not believe in an imperial ministry of the clergy with their conscious minds, but this may be a relic of a concept they need to move beyond. Or at least examine.

More on this theological point later. It is an important distinction in what "the process" is all about.

## What Goes On in the Congregation between Pastors

Some of what happens between pastors is becoming very familiar. More and more we are aware of the strong attachments that develop between pastor and people during a pastorate. They may be attachments of affection and deep relationship, or they may also be attachments of disappointment or even bitterness. But the attachments tend to be strong, not easily forgotten. Pastorates have some of the relational qualities of a marriage—both partners are marked and changed by a good marriage or even by a bad one.

What has become second nature to us is the realization that one does need a bit of time to grieve the loss of one relationship before one is able to enter another. Many clergy I know understand and appreciate the need for the congregation to have some space between pastors.

"But why so much?" is what I hear. "Isn't three or four months plenty of time?"

I find the concern also stated as suspicion about why interim pastors are needed. "Are those people just feathering their nests?" I hear. "Why wait a year?"

To understand the congregation's side of what is going on calls for walking through the steps that occur during a search. We have identified eight distinct events that occur between the leaving of one pastor and the successful installation of the next. Let me first identify and explain them briefly.

## a) Termination

Termination refers to a complex set of events and activities surrounding the leaving of the former pastor. This is often a highly emotional time for the congregation, and it is a time in which the former pastor is often out of sync with the congregation. The former pastor is struggling with a lot of dynamics of letting go and leaving, anticipating the new relationships lying ahead, thinking of the new place and people. The old place often feels rejection, anger, and bitterness. (Ten years ago when we studied clergy firing we used the euphemism "involuntary termination" to make it more palatable to talk about. When we asked lay people to talk about involuntary terminations they had seen in the church, I was shocked by one reply in its truth and also in how it exposed my own clericalism: "Most involuntary terminations I have experienced have been clergy telling the congregation they were leaving. The congregation was terminated, not the pastor!") The congregation often feels hurt. Pastors often do not help the congregation. (See Oswald's *Running Through the Thistles*,[1] a guidebook for those clergy who are leaving.)

## b) Direction-Finding

Congregations, particularly the leadership group and very especially the senior lay person, face anxiety that approaches panic when a pastor announces departure and actually departs. Often they do not know what procedures to follow. They probably have counted on the pastor to maintain relationships with the denomination, so they often do not know whom to call and whom to trust. They have to make those connections, learn what is laid down by denominational policies or customs. They have a lot to learn in a short time. They discover that there is a thing called interim pastors and another called consultants, and they have to make decisions about them. They have to figure out how to put together a search committee and plan what it is to do. They have to redo the annual budget to take into account new activities and needs. One of the more difficult tasks is being sure that the relationship with the former pastor is concluded, that future relationships with him or her are understood and clear, and that the former pastor's information on the parish is captured for future use.

## c) Self-Study

The self-study phase of the work is sometimes quite as elaborate as a long-range planning process. The energy required is substantial for even simpler systems. Some community analysis is often included. Self-studies generally produce a document that is a self-description of the congregation. The strength or weakness of the document or profile relates to the abilities of those who put it together. Sometimes congregations "let it all hang out"; more often at least some of the truth gets stated in the most favorable light. A congregation that has been in real difficulties may have a hard time putting it all out for public view. Clergy receiving these profiles need to read them with open minds. I have come to see them as "the best clues that parish is able to give about who they are at this time." Clergy sometimes seem to think these are supposed to be infallible documents and get offended when they discover that the reality turns out to be different from the description. Clergy need to know that the profile is a working document, the product of a flawed group of people trying to say something they can live with about themselves. I am sometimes astonished at the ability of congregations to speak difficult truth in these profiles, but I have learned not to be fundamentalistic in dealing with them.

## d) Search

Toward the end of the self-study, search committees start trying to translate what they see themselves to be (the profile) into the characteristics they think they need in their new clergyperson. Sometimes that develops into a formal job description. This is the point at which clergy candidates begin to hear directly from the congregation. They want to know who should be on their list, and generally they do not know whether there will be two or three or thirty or forty. (All too often congregations with eroded self-confidence cannot believe that anyone would ever come to them!) When they get fifty or sixty replies, many of them are simply overwhelmed with paper. If they have not yet done so, they have to stop and figure out how to manage all the data. What to file and how to respond. Usually this is being done by volunteers who never did anything quite like this before. Some things fall between cracks. A system is developed to "cull" the list according to things the congregation feels to be important. Those who do not seem to fit the job description get dropped. Those who don't fit for other reasons are dropped. The search committee's focus remains on those still in the list, which means that they sometimes forget to pay attention to those they have dropped. Most congregations intend to have a fail-safe procedure to let people know, but reality falls short of that. (To put it in perspective, who knows of an every member canvass by leaders of any congregation that doesn't manage to lose the names of the last twenty or thirty who are supposed to be contacted for a pledge? We need to remember that this system is driven by the same people and the same dynamics. That doesn't excuse it, it just states what we often forget.)

Clergy who get past the filing system experience the search phase more directly. They may have visits from teams and/or they may be invited to visit the congregation. When you are lucky, the interviewing is done by well-trained and rehearsed people who have thought through what they want to learn and communicate. That is not always the case— particularly if the congregation is not using a consultant. Clergy who want a good hearing for themselves should prepare themselves for well-run interviews, but be prepared with alternatives. In any case, this is a time at which your own skills and style can be communicated.

One word of caution. The worst thing that can happen is that anybody makes a fraudulent sale. If anxiety on the part of either makes the two parties collude with each other not to face facts, both will be losers. The best outcome is for each to communicate clearly what they are and what they are not. It is not worth it for the clergyperson to get the job, then for both to discover that they misread each other.

### e) and f) Decision and Negotiation

I name these two together because they often seem interwoven. It is important for both tasks to be accomplished: that congregation and candidate come to clear decisions and that the two negotiate how the relationship is to be carried out. Again, the congregation has had little experience doing this and they may not be experts. Different congregations have their own ways of formalizing agreements. Some want a "contract," some a "covenant," some a letter of agreement. Clarity is needed; the form in which it is cast may vary. Usually judicatories have at least a minimum requirement that protects both parties. Clergy would be well advised to talk over the agreement with a friend or colleague just to be sure. Sometimes anxiety about a job makes us overlook things we ought not overlook. It is also true in most cases that there is usually a fair amount of flexibility at this point—nobody is trying to put something over on anybody. If they are, you are already in trouble!

One unfortunate fact we find all too often is that once the decision is made, the congregation forgets the other candidates. With no real malice intended, they just get so excited about what has happened that they forget to let the unsuccessful candidates know. Most denominational executives and bishops and most consultants do their very best to see that this base is covered, but sometimes it does not happen or it happens too late. It is easy to understand why, but it is mighty hard for the person who waits by the telephone for the call that never comes.

A number of unsuccessful candidates really want to know why they were not chosen. Bolles gives some good suggestions about how to get feedback, but one must also be sensitive to the fact that some congregations or people really are not prepared to give that feedback. For one thing it is not something they do in ordinary life—unsuccessful candidates for jobs are told that they were turned down, but few are told the reasons.

### g) Installation

The installation is a terribly important symbolic act for the clergyperson and the congregation. But the clergyperson needs to recognize the incredible load of stress he or she is under. The congregation has had quite a while in which to get over its grief, but the pastor not only suffers family dislocation, but generally leaves one set of relationships with a great wrench one Sunday and walks into the next set of relationships the next week. Not surprisingly, such clergy are soon targets for criticism: "All she does is talk about her old parishioners and how they did things there." Clergy need to take care of their own need to grieve and not lay it all on the new congregation.

### h) Start-Up

The first 12-18 months in the new congregation are, we at Alban believe, critical in the establishment of the new pastorate. I will not go into detail on this beyond making the point that getting the job and getting on site does not mean the pastorate is yours. There is a dynamic period of relationship building and testing that must occur. We hope every judicatory provides resources for this start-up time. In our experience, neither the congregation nor the pastor are experts at it, yet unless the start-up is well done, the pastorate will be less than it could have been.

# Why It Takes Time

My hunch is that an efficient congregation could accomplish all the tasks listed above in four months. If they took a lot of shortcuts they might get it done in three. If they asked somebody else to do it for them, they might well have the pulpit filled the day the old pastor left.

The question is: What does one want to happen? If the task is to get a warm body in place as fast as possible, the shortest way is best. Often clergy, locked into anxiety about jobs, are tempted to this point of view.

If, however, the long-term concern is to build a pastor-congregation relationship that has the most potential for leading to a new dimension of ministry for each, we are talking about something quite different.

We have come to identify five distinct areas that need to be dealt with if such a relationship is to be built. We have come to call them "The Developmental Tasks of a Congregation in Search of a Pastor." (They are more fully described in my *Critical Moment of Ministry*.[2])

**The Five Developmental Tasks**

### 1. Coming to Terms with History
We see the period between pastors as a moment when the people of the congregation can come to terms with what lies in their past. Part of that means grieving the loss of their previous pastor. It may also involve coming to terms with ancient feuds or with the image of a great pastor of a generation ago. Many of the events listed above can be the arena in which this developmental task is done. The self-study should include not only the generation of statistical data but also personal conversations about the past, the heroes and heroines of earlier generations. It is a time of getting in touch with the identity of the congregation and celebrating it —but also freeing the people not to be in bondage to it. Well done, this developmental task will leave the congregation ready to move into a future.

### 2. Rediscovery of the Larger Church
The period without a pastor gives the congregation an opportunity to ex- perience the denomination and the judicatory office, to look critically at other congregations and how ministry is done there. It exposes the con- gregation's leaders to outstanding clergy from other parts of the country. It broadens their horizons and also makes them more cognizant of their

denominational heritage. A congregation should come out of this time recommitted to that heritage and ready to follow a pastor loyal to that heritage.

### 3. Emergence of New Leadership
The period after the previous pastor leaves is a prime time for the emergence of new lay leadership and for shifts of responsibility among the old leadership. Almost all the activities listed above give opportunity for the involvement of new leaders. A congregation conscious of the opportunity can give some leaders a chance to move out of roles they assumed with the old pastor. It also gives them a chance to search out those who just never happened to be called on or others who felt little attraction to working with the previous pastor. A congregation that takes advantage of this time can come out with a new cadre of leaders ready to work with a new pastor.

### 4. New Sense of Identity
The activities during this period can help a congregation trade in an old image of what they are and what their community is like for a new understanding of who they are and what God is calling them to become. There will be hints of that in the profile, but it is more than that. The lay leaders will—as they move through this period—discover some new confidence in themselves. They will get a new sense of what they can do and want to do. The better they look at their community, of course, the better they will be looking at the new context of their ministry and the more they are likely to feel that they are being pulled toward new opportunities to serve.

### 5. Commitment to New Directions and a New Leader
The end product of all these activities and developmental tasks is summarized here: our goal is not a warm body in a new job, it is a people committed to ministry and ready to move on it, a people eager to enter into relationship with a new leader who will help them in that new ministry.

## Summary: Theological Comment

Finding challenging positions for clergy is not an exact science. Splendid matches between clergy and congregations have been made by all kinds of unconventional systems. Indeed, what has been described here is not a system—it is a framework of activities that is carried out in a thousand different ways, depending on the gifts of those in the particular congregation.

Each clergyperson has the responsibility of developing her or his own abilities, gifts, and skills and working to see that those are invested in a ministry situation in which they are best used.

Each congregation, on the other hand, has the responsibility for engaging its people in their own nurture and growth and in commitment to ministry and mission where they are. Where it is possible, those congregations need to find ordained leaders who can lead them in those tasks.

I am convinced that ministry is grounded in and launched from community. This whole approach presumes that God's ministry and mission are active through that congregational community and that professional leadership of the community is an extraordinary gift the churches have developed to strengthen and enhance the community and the ministry and mission it produces. But this approach also presumes that where there is no resident professional leader, extraordinarily important work of ministry and mission goes on. Indeed, this approach presumes that some things happen best when there is a space in which the professional leadership is not present.

## Conclusion

Next time you find yourself waiting for a telephone call about a candidacy and nothing seems to be happening, try to relax.

The truth may be that a lot is happening, a lot that is out of your sight and also out of your experience. And if it is happening effectively and thoroughly, even if it is taking a longer time than you want it to, the intent is that the ground is being prepared for a far finer ministry than could have been without that work. The next pastor in that congregation may have a better chance to see new ministry emerge in her or himself and in the congregation.

Nothing is happening?

A lot may be happening.

NOTES

1. Roy M. Oswald, *Running Through the Thistles, Terminating a Ministerial Relationship with a Parish* (Washington, D.C.: The Alban Institute, Inc., 1978).

2. Loren B. Mead, *Critical Moment of Ministry: A Change of Pastors* (Washington, D.C.: The Alban Institute, Inc., 1986).

# The Clergy Job-Hunt Check List

*by Loren B. Mead*

This is a very simple tool to help clergy who are considering seeking a job change or who are planning one. Use these suggestions as a starting place, but also use your imagination and go beyond these.

| When | What To Do | How and Where |
|---|---|---|
| All is going well. You feel good about what you are doing. | Pay attention to your job and find ways to do it better. Work at expanding your skills and deepening your personal and spiritual life. Get feedback. Keep up to date on what's happening in the denomination, in society. | Continuing education. Spiritual direction. Read. Build networks of people who challenge you. Build a colleague group. Keep your dossier or profile current. |
| When all is well, but you wonder if you have stayed long enough. | Pay attention to your job. Investigate longer study leave possibilities. Get medical check-up. Be close to colleagues and advisors. Look out for feeling ambivalent, getting stuck in indecision. If you hear yourself asking "I wonder if I've stayed long enough—should | Go to career center to re-inventory skills, etc. Talk to executive or bishop and ask advice. Update your dossier with the denomination. Go to seminar on long pastorates. |

I stay or go?" take it as a sign to take responsible action such as that suggested in the next column.

**If you take a sabbatical...**

Plan it carefully with someone who will push you to be clear. Don't over-program. Plan the exit and re-entry. Engage the congregation as participant; design ways for them to experience it as a time of learning, too. Be sure your home situation is in good hands. After the sabbatical, treat your re-entry with all the care you would use in starting a new job.

Begin planning at least a year ahead. Use a consultant with yourself, with the parish. Get advice from others. Look over Alban publications on sabbaticals and starting up again.

**If you decide you should seek another position...**

Be very sure to keep your own current job on track. Do your job. Get as clear as you can about what you need to be and what you want to do—and where you want to do it.

Read Bolles' *What Color Is Your Parachute?* Do what he suggests. Use a career center. Activate your network of friends and colleagues. Be sure to do all the things your denomination provides—but don't depend solely on that. Talk to your Exec. or bishop. Use the phone. Go to meetings. Be sure your resume or profile is up to date.

If you get a nibble or inquiry...

Pay attention to your own job and people. *They* may get nervous. Respond promptly to what the inquiring church asks —watch out for overkill, for "selling." Do research on *them.* Find out if what they want connects with what you want to be or do. Watch out for being seduced by your need to "escape" or by a minor but attractive detail about them.

Use all the formal systems, but do not expect them to do the whole job. Talk to your denomination's linkage people. Ask your network about them. Locate informal links ("Joe's wife's family goes to that church!") Work to be direct and clear. Keep your network active for support—and be sure they are there if you experience rejection (you are very likely to!). Use a friend or consultant to keep you honest— someone who can help you express your emotions but can help you not get jerked around by them.

The nibble becomes courtship.

Pay lots of attention to your current job and people. Work on being clear about who you are and what you want. Work on learning who they are and what they want. Be open and honest and clear. Help them to do the same by your questions and approach.

Plan what you need to communicate to them and design ways to do it. Decide what you need to know about them and find out how to find it out. Do not depend entirely on the formal documents, etc. Keep your support group engaged. Be sure you are clear about the church's schedule of action. When in doubt, ask.

| If a call is extended... | Pay careful attention to your current job and people. (Alban has helpful books on terminating a pastorate if you choose to leave.) If you have worked hard up to now the decision is probably almost clear. If you are choosing between two prospects, keep *both* aware of your decision timetable. (*Don't* leave people hanging with fuzzy messages.) | Check your decision with a colleague, with your bishop or Exec. —someone who will ask hard questions. Get help in negotiating Ullman's "Letter of Agreement," available from Clergy Deployment Office, 815 2nd Avenue, New York, NY 10017 can help. Keep in touch with your stress level —don't take on new things. |
| --- | --- | --- |
| If a call is *not* extended... | Pay especial attention to your current job. Expect to feel worse than you expected. It can hurt. Ask search committee for feedback, but don't be resentful if they do not respond. | Use friends, support group. Allow yourself plenty of debriefing. Have colleague or consultant help you analyze how it went and learn. Don't be surprised it you feel angry or depressed (read Kubler-Ross, *On Death and Dying*). |
| If you get several turn-downs and feel discouraged... | Pay attention to current job. Review possibilities of renewed commitment in current situation. ("No call" *may* be a call to | Keep your support group active. Use counselor if depressed. Seek career center help in looking at other options. Get |

stay!) Explore radical job-change.

You feel *desperate* (you may have only a few months left on salary, for whatever reason, and nothing turns up).

If you haven't already done it, check for secular opportunities that fit your skills. Hire friend/colleague for real self-examination and reality-testing. Keep doing the things you've been doing—making contacts, phone calls, etc. Be prepared to take temporary job or position. Avoid desperate decisions ("*Any* parish will do!")

congregation consultant to explore options where you are.

Career center skill analysis can be adapted to nonchurch jobs. Be prepared to seek therapy or other help to keep out of depres-sion. *Accept* personal support from those in your network who can give it. Recognize that some cannot—your situation can make others anxious.

## Some general comments:

1. One key thing is presupposed—that all through all of this the clergy-person is working at a relationship with the spouse for support and advice, but also because the spouse is integral to the decision.

2. Stay in touch with your spiritual roots. This is a time that can test your commitments, your faith, your spirit. You cannot allow yourself to get separated from your grounding. You are looking for a *call*, not a job.

3. Take your emotions seriously. Get help when you need it. Feelings of anger, depression, elation, envy are absolutely to be expected. If you accept their reality and deal with them, they won't push you around.

# The Alban Institute:
## *an invitation to membership*

The Alban Institute, begun in 1979, believes that the congregation is essential to the task of equipping the people of God to minister in the church and the world. A multi-denominational membership organization, the Institute provides on-site training, educational programs, consulting, research, and publishing for hundreds of churches across the country.

The Alban Institute invites you to be a member of this partnership of laity, clergy, and executives—a partnership that brings together people who are raising important questions about congregational life and people who are trying new solutions, making new discoveries, finding a new way of getting clear about the task of ministry. The Institute exists to provide you with the kinds of information and resources you need to support your ministries.

Join us now and enjoy these benefits:

CONGREGATIONS, The Alban Journal, a highly respected journal published six times a year, to keep you up to date on current issues and trends.

**Inside Information,** Alban's quarterly newsletter, keeps you informed about research and other happenings around Alban. Available to members only.

**Publications Discounts:**

☐ 15% for Individual, Retired Clergy, and Seminarian Members
☐ 25% for Congregational Members
☐ 40% for Judicatory and Seminary Executive Members

**Discounts on Training and Education Events**

Write our Membership Department at the address below or call us at (202) 244-7320 for more information about how to join The Alban Institute's growing membership, particularly about Congregational Membership in which 12 designated persons receive all benefits of membership.

**The Alban Institute, Inc.**
**4125 Nebraska Avenue, NW**
**Washington, DC 20016**

DEMCO